D1256149

THE PALACES OF INDIA

THE PALACES OF INDIA

MAHARAJA OF BARODA

WITH PHOTOGRAPHS BY

VIRGINIA FASS

The Vendome Press
New York, Paris, Lausanne

Library of Congress Cataloging in Publication Data
Fatesinghrao Gaekwad, Maharaja of Baroda, 1930-
    The Palaces of India

Bibliography: P.
    1. Palaces – India. 1. Fass, Virginia. 11. Title.
NA1501.F34   954   80-51187

ISBN 0-86565-007-1

First edition 1980
Second impression 1985
Set in Monotype Garamond
Designed by Banks and Miles, London
Maps drawn by Peter Taylor
Made and Printed in Italy by
New Interlitho, Milan

CONTENTS

FOREWORD

With the publication of this book a long-cherished dream becomes a reality. When the idea first occurred to me a little research surprisingly revealed that this subject had never been tackled before. Scores of books are available on and about the princes of India, both historical and fictional, and yet I must hasten to add that although this book contains a brief historical introduction on the dynasties concerned, strictly speaking it is not a book on the princes. This is a humble attempt at leaving for posterity a record in words and photographs of the beautiful buildings they built and lived in and in which were housed carefully chosen, priceless art treasures both foreign and indigenous.

Had this been undertaken say thirty or forty or even perhaps fifty years ago, when these royal houses were at the height of their splendour, photographic results would have been even more breath-taking. All the same, I think I have been lucky even to have been able to catch a glimpse of them in their twilight. Indian Independence in 1947 was quickly followed first by the political and then by the territorial integration of most of the princely states with India – a happening as inevitable as the birth of dawn after a night. Final touches were given in December, 1971, bringing to an end all that remained of princely India. Adaptation to a totally new way of life became mandatory for survival. Pomp and splendour were shed, the Royal Elephant and the loyal retainer through no fault of their own met the same fate, and overnight these beautiful homes became White Elephants.

Today some of the palaces have been converted into hotels, some house government offices, some institutions, but many stand neglected and on the verge of ending as heaps of rubble. And yet, if the Government of India would wake up in time, many of them would have a chance of surviving as standing tributes to some of India's finest builders and craftsmen.

My dream began to take concrete shape some years ago after dinner one evening in London, and before I knew what was happening I had acquired both a photographer and a publisher.

In Virginia Fass I could not have found a better photographer. She completed the work of photographing forty palaces in thirty different places, during two trips to India, ably assisted by her elder sister Serena, herself no mean photographer, but who undertook the mundane job of taking down copious notes.

At that stage all I needed was the help of those of my brother princes whose palaces I had chosen for inclusion in this book. Their response to my appeal was spontaneous, and had it not been for their generosity and active co-operation this book could not have materialised.

The ball was now in my court. A great deal of research followed. Had I attempted to do this job alone, it would have taken me at least two more years to complete. But help came from two unforeseen quarters in the persons of Colonel Manohar Malgaokar, the well-known Indian novelist, and Dr Christopher Baker, Fellow and Tutor of Queens' College, Cambridge, who have rendered invaluable assistance.

This then is the brief historical background of this book. 'Sceptre and Crown must tumble down, and in the dust be equal made.' James Shirley's words have come true. The princes and princely India have finally departed from the Indian scene and henceforth shall only remain a part of Indian history. Tales of their deeds and misdeeds are all that are left for future generations. Even these beautiful palaces may one day no longer adorn the landscape, but I trust that this book will remain as a silent tribute and testimony to the aesthetic sense of those who created 'a thing of beauty' and who were great connoisseurs of art.

INTRODUCTION

In 1858 Queen Victoria became Empress of India, but she did not become the sole ruler of India. Nearly half of the territory of the subcontinent was still governed by Rajas, Maharajas, Maharawals, Nizams, Nawabs and others of exotic royal title. Seven hundred of such rulers commanded princely states that ranged in size from a few dusty acres to eighty thousand square miles, the equivalent of the British Isles. They had all made treaties with the British, accepted their 'paramountcy', and could not prevent occasional interference in their governance. But they were still royal, and sovereign.

These were the 'Native Princes' of British India. Thirty of these ruling houses built palaces which figure in this book and ruled over a quarter of the area of the entire subcontinent. They were scattered all over India – on the great plains in the interior of the peninsula, along the edge of the northern mountains – but were especially concentrated to the west, in the swathe of country which runs down from the plains of the Punjab, through the hills and deserts of Rajasthan, to the rough uplands of Maharashtra. The history of princely India is the history of the Sikh, Rajput and Maratha peoples who inhabited these areas, and their collisions with the imperial aims of the Great Moghul and the East India Company.

Previous Emperors of India had been no more successful than Queen Victoria in bringing all of the subcontinent under their sway. Indeed some of the princely houses had watched successive Muslim empires come and go in India since the eleventh century, while some with rather more imagination could trace their dynastic history back even further to the age of Hindu and Buddhist empires.

The princely houses with such admirably long memories came mostly from the clans of Rajputs or 'sons of princes'. They were tall, sturdy and warlike men who dominated north-western India two thousand years ago. They claimed descent from the sun and moon, and the royal authority which went with it, but they also stood smack in the path of Muslim expansion. Mahmud of Ghazni swept down into the Punjab in the eleventh century and began seven hundred years of Muslim conquest and empire in north India. The Rajputs scattered to the north, west and south, and so formed into the clans which eventually nurtured several of the princely houses. The most successful were those who took refuge in the deserts and hills of central and western India. This was a poor area, scarcely attractive to the greedy imperialist, but perfect as a base for guerrilla resistance. The Rajput chiefs built forts on the rocky outcrops, raided the valleys to provide themselves with food and booty, and eventually made the area known variously as Rajwarra, Rajputana or Rajasthan – the land of princes.

Here they fought against the Muslim invader, and against one another. Indeed they fought so much, and drank so much at other times, that their famous historian Colonel James Tod thought that they must somehow be distantly related to the Scandinavians. Only the greatest and last of the Muslim imperial dynasties, that of the Moghuls, was able to bring them to heel. But even the Great Moghul was 'king of the plains and open roads only' and after fighting the Rajput princes to a standstill did not treat them as mere subjects, but made them his allies and employed them as his generals. The booty of Moghul military campaigns made the Rajput chiefs rich; the umbrella of Moghul rule gave them security against one another. The Rajputs came down from their forts and, at places like Udaipur, Jaipur, Alwar and Dungarpur, began to build resplendent palaces.

Yet it was a season of false security. The Moghuls used the Rajputs' help to attempt conquest of south India and thus ruined their empire by a *folie de grandeur*. Through the eighteenth century the Moghul Empire gradually fell apart. New warlords appeared all over India. Few had a genealogy as long as that of a Rajput house yet within two generations their use of the sword made it possible for them to claim a royal title.

Two sets of people figured strongly in this new stage of state-building – the Marathas and the Sikhs. The Marathas were peasants and shepherds from the hills of western India. They could boast little history of military prowess before the middle of the seventeenth century, but then Sivaji, the son of a Maratha in the Moghul service, raised a revolt against its governor of western India. Within a few years, the Muslims had been driven out and a shaky Maratha state had emerged. Then in the mid-eighteenth century Maratha generals surged up northwards, and founded new capitals far away from their homelands, at Indore, Gwalior and Baroda. They seemed on the point of replacing the battered Moghul Emperor on the throne of Delhi when, in 1761, they were suddenly stopped in their tracks by an Afghan adventurer, Ahmad Shah Abdali, on a looting expedition.

Meanwhile, up in the north-west, the peoples of the Punjab had fortified themselves with a new martial religion of Sikhism and had grown equally tired of Muslim dominion. They swept down out of the Himalayan foothills, threw the Moghul officials out of their fortresses, and set up house in new capitals like Patiala, Faridkot and Kapurthala. Towards the end of the century, the most ambitious Sikh general, Ranjit Singh, started to absorb these principalities into a larger state which might also bid to control the vacant empire of north India.

Others now joined in the rising tide of revolt. In central India the Jats, who had long been the backbone of the local peasantry, and the Rohilla Afghans, who had come in as mercenaries in the Muslim armies, started to show their displeasure at Moghul rule. In the south, Moghul viceroys such as the Nizam of Hyderabad began to think about independence, and ambitious soldiers like Hyder Ali in the Mysore army began to see the possibilities of a military coup. In the north the rulers of the little buffer states, which were strung all along the Himalaya chain and which kept the plainsmen apart from the rough peoples of the hills, began to think about the good life without Moghul tribute.

Yet suddenly the political kaleidoscope of eighteenth-century India was given an unexpected twist. In the midst of this chaos of emerging states and conflicting imperial ambitions, the British East India Company began to blunder, expensively and bloodily, towards the foundation of a new Indian empire.

The British conquest was a haphazard process which took almost a century to complete and which was no more successful than the Moghuls in subduing many of the rulers of local India. Some of the old princes and new warlords were blasted out of the pages of history by the Company artillery, but others were drawn into alliance and confirmed in their territories. The Maratha warlords were the Company's most consistent enemies, but in the end they were allowed to keep their states. The Sikh kingdoms on one side of the Sutlej river were blessed with British protection, while those on the other were chased back to the hills. The old Moghul viceroy in Hyderabad was allowed to take a domain which virtually spanned the peninsula, while similar viceroys in Bengal and the Carnatic (southern India) were reduced to the state of political pensioners. It seemed illogical, but it was the inevitable result of a settlement brought about by a handful of young British military officers who each had an army at his back, a sheaf of treaties in his hand, and a six-month sea-journey between him and his bosses in London. But there was a pattern. All in all, the British settlement was remarkably like that of the Moghuls. The imperial ruler controlled the coasts and rich territories like the Ganges valley and the plains of the far south, while the petty princes ruled the deserts, hills and uplands.

In the first half of the nineteenth century, the British dismantled the princes' armies, refereed their dynastic quarrels, and helped them to come to terms with peace; but mostly they left them alone. Yet in 1857 when the Bengal army revolted, the rulers of the Native states helped to keep some of the most lawless areas of India loyal and quiet. Many were immediately rewarded with medals, honours and resounding titles, and from then on the British took great care to associate the princes with the great ritual occasions of the Empire. Great Durbars (audiences) were staged in India so that the princes might preen themselves before visiting British monarchs. Special units were formed so that the martial talents of the princes might be harnessed to the assistance of the Empire. The heirs of princely rulers were carefully educated in utilitarian principles and encouraged to turn their feudal principalities into 'model states'. And the British urged the princely rulers to join with them in recreation; many of them had always hunted, some took easily to polo, cricket and other sports, and a few could even be persuaded to build ballrooms in their palaces.

The security of British rule made way for another phase of palace building. In the Maratha states of central India, in the Sikh principalities of the Punjab, in the southern states of Hyderabad and Mysore, in the hilly buffer-states of Tripura, Kashmir and Cooch Behar, and even in many of the old Rajput kingdoms of Rajasthan, new buildings sprang up to express the native rulers' ideas of their own prestige, to provide the facilities for dedicated jollification, and to indulge a taste for the luxuries which they could now afford.

But again it was a false sense of security. The British bowed to the forces of nationalism and, after a slight hesitation when they thought of using the princes as a fifth column in Indian politics, decided to leave India as quickly and gracefully as possible. Over their departing shoulder they urged their erstwhile princely allies to forget about the old concept of paramountcy and any obligations it might have bestowed on the British rulers, and to merge themselves with the emergent nations of India and Pakistan. In 1948 the princes were persuaded to give up their states yet remain as well-kept pensioners with fancy titles. In 1971 the Indian parliament took away the remains of their princely incomes and privileges. They are left with their history – and their palaces.

The palaces are an extraordinary legacy. India's typical building is the single-roomed hut. Besides the skyscrapers of the modern cities there are few buildings that rise above the second storey; and with a handful of notable exceptions even the religious buildings are small in size if elaborate in composition. But occasionally this stooping landscape is interrupted by a building of immense size and of fantastic architectural bravura. The palaces are a testament to the princes' power, wealth and capacity for self-indulgence.

They are also remarkably varied. There is a range of styles from the various regions of the huge subcontinent itself, and there are a variety of Islamic touches brought in by the Muslim invaders. But then the palaces covered in this book also include a Venetian merchant's mansion, a Louis XIV palace, an art deco fantasy, a *beaux arts* classical façade, a north Italian country villa and a copy of St Peter's Rome. Moreover, there are several brave attempts at hybridisation. India has always had a very open-minded culture. It has absorbed different races, religions and rulers and created from them its own very distinctive mixture. In the same way the palace-builders have absorbed Indian, Islamic and European styles and often produced unique attempts to blend the best of these various styles into a distinctive monument. To the architectural purist such buildings can only be regarded as gorgeous trash. But to their architects and their princely patrons they were no more and no less than a homage to the varied and colourful history which had created princely India.

The princes were men of war but they built their palaces in times of peace. Only when the seemingly incessant battling for territorial control was brought to a halt could the princes venture out of their forts and build rather more comfortable and luxurious residences. Such times of peace came when there was an overlord who could hold the clashing ambitions of the princes themselves in check. The Moghuls were able to do this, and so were the British.

There were thus two main phases of palace construction. The first came during the high point of Moghul rule from the late sixteenth to the early eighteenth century; and the second came in the heyday of the British Raj, in the late nineteenth and early twentieth centuries. It was ironic that the princes were only able to build monuments to their own royal grandeur when they themselves were subordinate to another imperial power, but it was also this irony that ensured that the princes would try to blend the architectural traditions of their own warrior pasts with a certain homage to the styles of their current overlords.

The first phase of palace-building is marked by a blend of local warrior styles with the Persian influences of the Moghul Empire. The princes who built in these years were exclusively the Rajputs, who gained wealth and prestige by serving as the military lieutenants of the Moghul Emperors. The interiors of their palaces had several features in common: they had one or two halls of audience, a set of apartments for the men of the household, stables and servants' quarters, and finally the women's apartments or *zenana*. However, there were two distinct ways in which these elements were arranged.

The first was a direct development from the castles which the Rajput warriors had just abandoned in order to build more sumptuous palaces. There was generally a single, monolithic building like a castle keep. On the exterior there were few windows and little ornamentation on the lower storeys, for such was the pattern of a fortified castle wall. But at the top these palaces broke out into a riot of canopies, kiosks, towers, ornamental turrets and crenellations which gave the effect of fantastical icing on a rather massive cake. The interior meanwhile was often quite dark and labyrinthine, with miles of gloomy corridors separating the different sections of the palace, and perhaps an occasional courtyard to admit air and light. This was the basic pattern for the palaces at Udaipur and at Bundi.

The second of these early types was directly descended from the forts which the Moghul Emperors built at Agra and Delhi. Rather than a single castle-like building there was an enormous wall enclosing several separate buildings often set in an ornate garden. The halls of audience were generally pillared pavilions. Many of the Rajput princes, including Jaipur, Dungarpur and Alwar, who had visited and admired the court of the Moghul Emperor, built palaces in this style.

The stylistic features and ornamental details of these palaces also blended some distinctively Rajput features with more clearly Moghul touches. Early Rajput architecture, as revealed in temples and forts which predate the Moghul influence, is distinguished by a simple trabeate style of construction; there is no attempt to build anything such as an arch, dome or buttress, so that the weight of the roof is laid off horizontally or diagonally rather than vertically downwards. This basic fact of design led to lavish use of corbelling techniques to create doorways, to give curves to walls, and to provide external decoration; and it also led to a profuse use of brackets which held up balconies and roofs, creating false arches in otherwise square trabeate doorways, and lending themselves to elaborate decoration. For ornament the Rajputs relied mostly on intricate carving; lotus flowers, elephants, serpents and dragons were favourite designs.

The most distinctive architectural addition of the Muslim invaders was the arch, and its three-dimensional counterpart, the dome. These shapes already had religious significance for the Muslim builders since they were characteristic parts of the architecture of the mosque, and when the Muslim invaders discovered that such shapes were not known in Hindu India, they became concrete symbols of Muslim domination. The Moghuls also brought a number of elements of interior decoration from a distinctly Persian tradition – notably inlay work in ivory, hardwood and precious stones, mirror-work using coloured glass and reflective metals, and a passion for smothering interior surfaces in a calculated chaos of geometrical patterns.

But though it is possible to point to some distinctive and separate features of Hindu-Rajput and Islamic-Persian architecture and decoration, the 'Moghul' style is an inextricable tangle of the two traditions. The Moghul designers may have come to India with their heads full of Persian ideas, but in India they found new working materials – notably the remarkably useful local sandstone which could take much more elaborate carving than any stones used in their native Persia – and were obliged to employ native Hindu craftsmen. Thus immigrant Muslim designers and native Hindu artisans worked together, probably quite fractiously, to produce a distinctive Moghul style. Nowhere is this more obvious than in the motifs of carved and inlaid decoration. According to strict Islamic norms, it was heresy to include representations of living beings in ornamental decoration, hence the Islamic passion for geometrical patterns. But in deference to the Hindu artisans, and to the Rajput wives taken by the Moghul princes and Emperors, Islamic standards were relaxed somewhat, and flowers and animals found their way in among the geometric shapes. On a wider scale this process produced a style of architecture and ornament which included carved brackets, elephants and lotus flowers on one side, domes, arches and inlay on the other, and which was neither Rajput nor Persian but distinctively 'Moghul'.

While most of the Rajput palaces of the early period are built according to some variant of this 'Moghul' pattern, the later phase of palace-construction during British rule shows evidence of a much wider range of influences. Unlike the Rajputs, who had a long history of princely endeavour, many of the other states which appeared in the eighteenth century had no clear tradition of monumental architecture of their own. The Marathas, for instance, had been peasants until the eighteenth century – their forts relied more on their inaccessible position than on any form of martial stonework; their only two palaces built before British influence became dominant were carved teak-wood structures at Poona and at Berar which were easily burnt down and were thus not widely copied.

Moreover, by the time the building of palaces began in earnest in the late nineteenth century, the British had firmly and deliberately extended their influence over princely India. The heirs to the princely thrones were being carefully educated under the auspices of European tutors and guardians, whisked off on tours of Europe so that their minds might be broadened beyond the world of court intrigue and sumptuous indulgence, and encouraged to join Europeans in the serious business of social recreation.

This brought about several important changes in the internal design of the palaces. The old halls of audience were now replaced by a Durbar hall which was not so much for the ruler to receive his subjects, but for the ruler to receive his British overlords or their ambassadors, with as many as possible of the state's nobles and retainers in resplendent attendance. The palace also needed guest rooms suitable for the European visitors, and facilities for their entertainment – a billiard room, a ballroom (the Durbar hall might sometimes double up for this), dining rooms, tennis courts, polo fields, shooting lodges and swimming pools.

With their new education and their new social function, the princes needed palaces with a new form of architecture and new feats of engineering. Some princes hired known European architects, many more used enterprising engineers from the British Indian Army, while others relied on their own, amateur doodles. Some of the architects strove to build careful reproductions of known styles – both Indian and European. There were some remarkably faithful reprises of the Moghul style, such as the palace at Bikaner. Then there were attempts at reproducing styles which were in vogue in Europe. The *beaux arts* classicism popular in late nineteenth-century France fed into the palace built at Kapurthala; the passion for Italianate Renaissance design found its way to Cooch Behar, Porbandar, Gwalior and Tripura. The civic classicism of early twentieth-century Britain finished up on a rock outside Jodhpur.

But many of the amateur architects and their patrons felt no compunction to stick to the canons of a single style, and for many of the professional architects the commission to build a princely palace conveyed a licence to break all the stylistic rules and to merge together a variety of favourite features into a distinctive and personal creation.

From these brave attempts at blending resulted two distinctive new styles. The first, known rather vaguely as Indo-Saracenic, was first used on many of the official buildings constructed by the Raj in the latter half of the nineteenth century and only later found its way into palace architecture. It was, supposedly, a blend of Indian and Islamic styles, though it was deliberately a different blend from the Rajput-Moghul hybrid. Such an effort of stylistic commingling could only be attempted by designers who belonged to neither of the constituent cultures, and indeed the most successful of the Indo-Saracenic architects was an English engineer, Charles Mant, who built the palaces at Kolhapur and Baroda.

The second of these new hybrid styles was never specifically christened but it might properly be called 'Renaissance Oriental'. Throughout the century, architects attempted to translate the building fashions of Europe to the Empire. At first they tried Gothic, but because this relied so heavily on the decorative qualities of windows, and because windows in India tended, if unguarded, to admit heat as well as light, many of the results of this effort of transposition were quite uninhabitable. 'The application of classic architecture to Indian buildings is attended with difficulties,' noted a speaker at the Royal Institute of British Architects in 1881, 'but the achievement of a successful Gothic building, under conditions which entail the concealment of its windows, is an even greater problem.' Someone suggested that the Gothic style might be rescued by sheltering the windows with a *verandah* constructed from a roofed row of flying buttresses, but unsurprisingly no-one seems to have taken this up. Instead, the fashion for Renaissance architecture, which anyway became more popular in Europe in the second half of the century, proved more easy to transport to the hotter climate.

Moreover, it was relatively easy to combine Renaissance features with elements of Indian, particularly Moghul, design. The two styles shared a taste for careful proportions, for domes, for colonnades, for friezes, for clusters of arches, and for tiered frontages with strong horizontal lines. Thus it was possible to create designs in which it was almost impossible to separate the Indian and European inheritances. Indore, Gwalior, Benares and Wankaner all emerged from this curiously intangible stylistic collision.

Finally there were some palaces where the demands of sumptuous grandiosity and the dictates of conspicuous display overtook any notions of stylistic accuracy, integrity or restraint. Such palaces mixed the colourfulness which had always marked Indian design with the widest possible variety of features robbed from every possible stylistic tradition. These were the result of orgiastic shopping sprees in the bargain basement of architecture. They were deliberately excessive but they were not necessarily out of place in the Indian landscape. Such palaces are a link in a long chain. They are modelled on notions of royal luxury and extravagance that run through the ancient Indian myths and folk-tales. And they now serve as backdrops for the colourful extravaganzas of India's cinema industry.

UDAIPUR

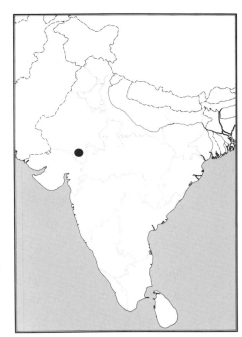

You can still live like a prince in India. There is a small island of cool marble set in a beautiful, placid lake amid the rugged mountains of Rajasthan. The island is in fact a summer palace. The marble walls enclose rooms which have been built for no purpose other than royal pleasure. The walls are painted sumptuously with elaborate friezes, haunting floral designs, hunting scenes, and images of dancing girls. The furniture ranges from the luxurious silk cushions favoured by the Indian nobleman to fantastic crystal furniture brought from the emporiums of Europe. The rooms are arranged around calm pools which reflect the brilliant blue of the enormous sky. From the terraces there is an unparalleled view across the shining lake towards the jumble of Udaipur town, a frieze of lakeside gardens, clusters of other palaces, and the dark rim of mountains beyond.

Outside – the whiteness of marble, luminous blue of the sky, stark brownness of mountain, reflective brightness of sun, sky and lake, the flashing colour of brilliant green birds; inside – the sensuousness and luxury of royal indulgence, carefully and expensively preserved.

You reach this sparkling creation not by the shiny limousine favoured by the princes in modern times, nor even by the stately elephants which carried the princes in the past. But by rowing boat. And you don't have to be a prince to enjoy this creation, merely a customer. The pleasure-haunt of the rulers of Udaipur is now the Lake Palace Hotel.

The three foremost among the Rajput states were Amber, which founded a capital at Jaipur; Marwar, which settled on Jodhpur; and Mewar, which built the city and palaces of Udaipur. Among them, Mewar laid claim to pre-eminence partly because it was the most ancient but mostly because of its history of fierce resistance to Muslim rule. It is a history that highlights the valour of the Rajputs, but also their mutual jealousies, and above all it is a history of human slaughter on a staggering scale.

The original capital was at Chittore, an enormous fortified rock in the hills of eastern Mewar. The Muslim invaders quickly realised the importance of this stronghold and three times they conquered it. On each occasion, the fort fell after a long resistance and the capitulation was marked by a grisly sacrifice. On the eve of battle, when all hope of victory had gone, the wives, daughters and concubines of the defenders burned themselves *en masse* in a rite known as *johar*. The following morning, the remaining Rajput warriors, drunk with opium, threw open the gates and fell on their attackers with the sole aim of taking as many of the enemy as possible with them to the grave. Once the Rajput warriors had fallen, the Muslim troops entered the fort and slaughtered everything that moved. This final orgy of destruction was also dignified with a ritual title – the *saka*.

The scale of these killings was horrifying. In the second of the *johar* as many as thirteen thousand women immolated themselves, and after

the third *saka* Akbar, the great Moghul Emperor, weighed the collars removed from the corpses and reached a figure translated as six hundred pounds.

In each case, however, the Mewar Rajputs took care to preserve the princely line and sent the ruler's son and heir off to a mountain retreat before the final massacre began. After the third *johar* the surviving prince, Pertap Singh, spent five years skulking in the Aravalli mountains and leading a fretful guerrilla resistance against the Moghul troops. The other two great Rajput houses of Amber and Marwar had by now come to a settlement with Akbar, had given their daughters to Moghul princes, and were now growing rich and important as the military officers of the Moghuls. But the Mewar Rajputs held out for a further half-century, refused to send a daughter to a Moghul bed, and came to no settlement with the Moghuls until 1612. Even then, the Mewar house of Udaipur was the first to raise the standard of revolt against the

The City Palace at Udaipur as seen from Lake Pichola.

Stone elephants salute those arriving at Jagmandir.

Moghuls at the end of the seventeenth century. When British rule was established, the Udaipur house still retained a studied aloofness: the Udaipur princes rarely bothered to travel outside their domain, shirked the great Imperial Durbars, never travelled to England, and refused to be pushed by the British into schemes of constitutional reform or economic development. Fateh Singh, who ruled Udaipur in the early twentieth century, refused even to set up a finance department, let alone initiate plans of agricultural or commercial improvement. 'I am Rajput,' he explained proudly, 'soldier and statesman. Not tradesman.'

This policy of defiant independence made the rulers of Udaipur the greatest of the Rajput houses and the acknowledged defenders of Rajput purity and honour. But unfortunately such pre-eminence helped to breed dissension in the Rajput ranks.

Because the Udaipur house had never entered into a marriage alliance with the Moghuls, the daughters of the Udaipur prince became especially sought after as brides. In 1807 the other two great Rajput houses of Jaipur and Jodhpur vied for the hand of the princess Krishna Kumari. The Udaipur ruler dithered and appeared to hold out some hope to both of the parties. Even though the independence of the Rajputs was threatened from all sides – by the Maratha generals, by the British troops, by the Pindari bandits who roamed central India in the wake of the Maratha armies, and by their own recalcitrant nobles – Jaipur and Jodhpur prepared to go to war with one another for the hand of Krishna Kumari and the prestige of an Udaipur match. To prevent this disaster Krishna Kumari calmly committed suicide through poison. It was an act in the great tradition of Rajput female sacrifice and it brought forth a cruel and callous witticism from a bored East India Company official in Calcutta: 'Women should die young and by violent means, if they desire the reputation of their beauty to live with posterity. Her story deserves well to be commemorated in a Melodrama.'

An arched window in a bedroom of the City Palace. The cusped or 'peacock' arch was a characteristic feature of Rajput decoration.

Mirror-work set into plaster in a Moghul design on the walls of the City Palace.

Red and silver mirror-work on the walls of a state bedroom in the City Palace.

Chinese tiles face the walls and ceiling of a bedroom in the City Palace. The niches were for oil lamps. The doorway and the niches replicate the arches of the window opposite.

LEFT *A fresco in the apartments of the City Palace. Elephants in ceremonial dress wash themselves in a lily pond.*

Murals at the entrance to the royal apartments in the City Palace depict the arrival of the bridegroom at a royal marriage.

Amidst this turbulent history emerged the startling city-palace of Udaipur. The surviving prince Pertap Singh died five years after the third sack of Chittore in a hut in the Aravalli mountains with the words: 'These sheds will give way to sumptuous dwellings thus generating the love of ease; and luxury with its concomitants will ensue, to which the independence of Mewar, which we have bled to maintain, will be sacrificed.' Although he was still lamenting his exile from the Chittore fortress, he had in fact found the spot where his successors would raise the great city of Udaipur and his words had a prophetic quality. Although the new site did not have the grandeur of the great Chittore rock, it was a very good defensive retreat – a small, wooded plain hidden in the mountains. It already had one natural lake; when some carefully built dams created several more it became not only hospitable and beautiful but also very easy to defend: only three passes remained down to the valleys below. The Emperor Jahangir failed to breach the defences.

The Peacock Courtyard in the City Palace.

The palaces were built largely in the seventeenth century. The crucial precondition was a settlement with the Moghuls which reduced the threat of invasion, and this new friendliness with the Moghuls is reflected in the influence of Moghul decoration. Jagat Singh, ruler of Udaipur from 1628 to 1654, in fact was very friendly with the Emperor Shah Jahan and allowed his workmen to copy some of the glories of his incomparable buildings at Agra. Later when Shah Jahan's bigoted son and successor, Aurangzeb, dismissed his Hindu craftsmen, several of them found employment at Udaipur.

The Sajjan Nivas or Lotus Suite in the Lake Palace. The murals show girls dancing among lotus leaves.

Thus the Udaipur city-palace is a blend of Moghul decorative art and Rajput military architecture. It is sited on a hill beside the Pichola lake and strives, through its sheer length, bulk and elevation, to recall the huge, tall, flat and fortified rock of Chittore. It is simply enormous – a jumble of not one but of at least four separate palaces covering some four acres and exceeding all the other princely palaces for colossal grandeur. When the lakeside hill ran out of space it was artificially extended by terraces supported on huge stone arches. The exterior is built of thin slates of sandstone, backed by rubble and brickwork on the more solid elevations, and covered with the finest possible white plasterwork. Like a fort, its exterior walls are steep and undecorated – particularly impressive where they rise out of the lake – and most of the external flourishes are confined to the riot of domes, arches, turrets, crenellations and kiosks on the roof.

But while the exterior recalls the might of Chittore, the interior records the admiration of Moghul Delhi. In the principal rooms, marble is virtually the only building material, and every conceivable surface is decorated with inlay, painting and mosaics in the geometric and florid patterns which the Moghuls brought from Persia. There are frescoes depicting the history of Mewar and turrets copied from the battlements

The lily pond in the courtyard of the Lake Palace.

The Khush Mahal or Happiness Suite, now favoured by Indian honeymooners.

Belgian crystal furniture dating from 1820. Such pieces became very popular with the princely families in the nineteenth century.

of Chittore, but the predominant effect is achieved through coloured glass, mirror-work, fluted marble columns copied from Shah Jahan's throne in the Agra fort, pavilions and fountains on the Moghul model; and marble everywhere.

Other influences creep in to compete with the Rajput and the Moghul. In the mid-nineteenth century the ruler Sirdar Singh built a Khush Mahal, or palace of pleasure, to receive his European guests, and this includes an enormous chandelier to vie with the profusion of mirror-work in reflecting the light. Here and there a Rajput silver door has been surrounded by blue-and-white tiles from China. In many places the mixture of Rajput styles, second-hand Moghul work and nineteenth-century European and exotic additions threatens to overwhelm the conception. But most visitors have looked kindly on this cacophony. A nineteenth-century French traveller wrote that:

'One of the rooms, decorated in a grotesque and fanciful manner, would excite

23

the amusement of a European stranger; yet in reality, it is scarcely more ridiculous than the China galleries at Fontainebleau and elsewhere. The walls of the rooms are ornamented with European plates, cups and saucers; the commonest pottery side by side with the finest Dresden; Bohemian glass next to a trumpery salt-cellar.'

In the lake itself, and on the hills beyond, are other palaces. Jagmandir, which was built for a Moghul prince seeking refuge from his father and who later went on to become the Emperor Shah Jahan and the friend of Udaipur, is a cluster of pavilions and palaces, set in a Moghul-style garden and apparently floating on the surface of the lake. But the most famous is the delicate white island which now houses the most famous hotel in India. Once it was the refuge of the Rajput nobles, enjoying the 'love of ease' that the fugitive Pertap Singh had foreseen:

'Here they listened to the tales of the bard, and slept off their noonday opiate

amidst the cool breezes of the lake, wafting delicious odours from myriads of the lotus flower which covered the surface of the waters; and as the fumes of the potion evaporated, they opened their eyes on a landscape to which not even its inspirations could frame an equal . . . Amid such scenes did the princes and chieftains recreate during two generations, exchanging the din of arms for voluptuous inactivity.'

Jagmandir in the Pichola Lake. This water-garden palace acted as sanctuary for the future Moghul Emperor, Shah Jehan, when he rebelled against his father.

Amidst the dissensions of the Rajput tribes, and the voluptuousness of the once-martial aristocracy, Udaipur was sacked by the Marathas in 1804, and had no time to recover before it was overtaken by the stultifying security of British rule. The plaster is now peeling, the mosaic and inlay looks a bit careless and over-ornate, the massiveness seems gross, and the confusion of style becomes oppressive. But Udaipur is still salvaged by its history and its conception – a gaudy monument to the hedonistic excess brought on by a surfeit of warring.

25

The main gateway to the compound of the Jaipur palace was built tall enough to admit a procession of elephants.

JAIPUR

Jaipur has style. First, a long crenellated wall and two stout bastions. All pink. Beyond, wide boulevards flanked by busy bazaars. Silversmiths, perfume-sellers, embroiderers and horse-dealers; camels jostling with crowded three-wheeled minibuses. The skyline is a mass of roofs and façades – square, domed, stepped, crenellated – but all pink. The palace is right at the centre of the city, and the series of gateways that admit the visitor into this vast complex are all pink – even down to the guardian elephants. And finally a mass of pillars, kiosks, colonnades and niches: some are marble; some are made of the finest white *chunam* plaster; some are painted and inlaid in a blaze of different colours. But most are pink.

Compared to Udaipur, Jaipur is spiritually and geographically much closer to Delhi. Udaipur is secluded in the hills; but Jaipur stands on one of the main routes from Delhi to Bombay. The Udaipur palace's homage to Moghul overlordship is a bit grudging – the dainty Moghul decorations are rather overwhelmed by the mass of martial stonework – but the Jaipur palace espouses the culture of Moghul Delhi in a much more wholehearted way.

This difference of architectural tastes reflects the contrast in the two states' responses to the Moghul intrusion. While Udaipur resisted long and nobly, the house of Amber (for that was the original capital of the Jaipur rulers) maintained its stature and its independence through collaboration. Amber was the first of the Rajput families to marry a princess to a Moghul Emperor, to provide a general for the Moghul armies, and to be rewarded with the *cachet* of a high Moghul title.

Thus the family became rich and privileged, and outgrew its old capital in the hills. In 1728, they moved from the old fort of Amber, and founded a new city seven miles away in the flat bed of a dried-up river. Thus Jai Singh II founded Jaipur.

It was more than a simple change of locale. The house of Amber had already begun to lose its pre-eminence at the Moghul court, and predatory neighbours had already begun to claw back the territories which Amber had gained through its Moghul alliance. In place of warfare, the Jaipur rulers turned to more cultured pursuits. This change was very much the work of Jai Singh II and it is clearly reflected in the city which he founded.

Jai Singh II was an engineer, architect, town planner, art collector, mathematician, astronomer, inventor, and a lover of good living and good music. He laid out Jaipur as a carefully planned city influenced both by the traditional canons of Hindu architecture and by a concern for hygiene, beauty and prosperity. The city is arranged on a grid, defined by wide avenues, orientated to two temples on the surrounding hills, and focused on the palace at its heart. There were streets for different sets of traders and craftsmen, and an ordered variety of architectural decorations. Although it is now so famous as the 'Pink City' it was

The City Palace at Jaipur was built in the early eighteenth century. The variety of different arch shapes, picked out on the pink-painted walls, are characteristic of late-Rajput decoration.

originally painted in a variety of colours and only in the nineteenth century repainted so that virtually all the buildings matched the pink sandstone used in some of the palaces and other substantial constructions. In the palace complex, which is something of a city itself, there are not only the usual accoutrements of an Indian royal residence, but also an astronomical observatory. Jai Singh II was passionate about astronomy, found inaccuracies in the studies of contemporary astronomers in Europe, translated Euclid, and reformed the lunar calendar. In memory of his family's past services, the Moghul Emperor made Jai Singh II a governor of the rich and important province of Agra, though in fact he used this opportunity not to increase his tribute but to spray north India with more astronomical observatories, including the one that still stands near the heart of New Delhi.

The palace complex itself is the most daring and successful synthesis of Moghul and Rajput styles. The Moghul influence comes not only in

The entrance to the private apartments in the City Palace is guarded by a pair of marble elephants and a troupe of smartly dressed retainers.

the interior detail as at Udaipur and elsewhere, but also in the basic layout of buildings. As in the Moghul forts of Agra and Delhi, so in the Jaipur palace the buildings designed for different functions stand separately in a neat geometrical garden, with the whole complex surrounded by high walls. Further, many of the buildings are quite small, often single-storeyed and open to the breeze like a Moghul pavilion.

But it is a conception that has been used and modified in an idiosyncratic way. For there is also much in the palace which recapitulates the design of the Rajput fortresses and much which owes more to several centuries of Hindu religious and secular architecture than to the comparatively recent admixture of Moghul ideas. As in the Amber fort, one progresses towards the centre of the Jaipur palace complex through a series of buildings each in turn dedicated to an increasingly private function. The stables and administrative offices succeed to the guest house, then come the hall of public audience, the hall of private

More decorative arches in the main courtyard of the City Palace. The peacock provides the dominant motif.

audience, the treasury and subsidiary royal apartments, and finally the royal residence – the Chandra Mahal or Moon Palace – and its luxurious garden. The two halls of audience are built in a clear Moghul style and the guest house or Mubarak Mahal (built after Jai Singh's time) owes much to the buildings of the deserted Moghul capital at Fatehpur Sikri near Agra. But many of the details owe nothing to the Moghuls at all. The square gateways topped with a gatehouse, the ornate brackets holding up delicate balconies, the profusion of carved friezes and the recurrence of motifs based on the lotus flower and the spear-head are designs which run through north Indian Hindu stone architecture from its earliest surviving traces. When one finally reaches the main palace or Chandra Mahal, one finds a building which could never have survived in a Moghul fort. It is a seven-tiered, vaguely pyramidical structure designed to ensure shelter from the sun and access to the breeze. (There is an earlier version of this distinctly Rajput design that can still be detected in the ruins of the old palace in the Chittore fort.)

The Sheesh Mahal or Hall of Mirrors in the upper storey of the main royal apartments. These luxurious rooms were built in most of the Rajput Palaces.

After the success of Jai Singh's architectural panache, later Jaipur rulers have crammed the city and its surrounds with many more palaces. The Ram Bagh palace was the work of the nineteenth-century ruler, Ram Singh, who kept alive Jai Singh's enthusiasm for architecture that was both beautiful and functional, and who helped turn Jaipur into the comfortable capital of a progressive state. Ram Bagh's most famous occupants, however, were Man Singh and Madho Singh who copied Jai Singh's ebullient eccentricity rather than his architectural creativity. Madho Singh was originally denied the *gadi* or throne of Jaipur by an ambitious half-brother, and promptly retired to the hills to become an outlaw. He reformed slightly after meeting a holy man who predicted that he would succeed to the throne, and indeed in 1880 his former rival died and bequeathed it to him. This stroke of fortune completed his transformation from rough bandit to orthodox prince. While ruler of Jaipur he prohibited the slaughter of all animals within ten miles of the city and as a result the whole tract was overrun with wild boar, deer and

The Rambagh Palace, now a luxurious hotel. The lotus-leaf fountain is made of marble.

stray dogs. He agreed to attend King Edward's coronation in London, but took with him a six-month supply of Ganges water to counter the polluting effect of the sea-journey.

He spent a youthful year in England and returned a convinced Anglophile, bringing back an English cook and English furniture. 'His Prime Minister,' noted a European guest, 'has introduced English herbaceous borders into Jaipur.' Man Singh was also a fanatical polo player, with the result that Ram Bagh was distinguished as the only private residence in the world with its own polo field – besides the usual complement of tennis and squash courts and an indoor swimming pool. When a broken arm prevented him from playing polo he learnt to fly, and built his own private aerodrome.

Ram Bagh is now a hotel and so is another royal residence, the glistening white Jai Mahal. Besides these palaces there is also the Roopniwas, hidden in the defile leading up to Amber; the Sisodia Maharani's palace, another tiered palace running down to a bathing place in the hills; and the Moti Doongri, an exact replica of a Scottish castle, lurking incongruously among dark trees on the heights above the city.

But the most extraordinary of this extraordinary collection is the Hawa Mahal or Palace of the Winds. It is not really a palace, but a façade built on to the walls of Jai Singh's original palace by a successor, Pertap Singh. The first two storeys are backed by a basement and courtyards, but the three storeys above consist only of passages and balconies. It was designed to give the inmates of the palace an airy

Hawa Mahal, or Palace of the Winds, is a façade built onto a wall of the main palace compound. Royal ladies seated in its 953 niches and windows could look down on processions in the main street below without compromising *their* purdah.

ABOVE *Rear view of the top of the façade.*

33

An eighteenth-century silver urn for storing the sacred water brought from the river Ganges.

One of a pair of elephants guarding the royal apartments in the City Palace shows the skill of Jaipur's famous stone-carvers

retreat from which they could view the town below. Although at first the structure looks somewhat like a Hollywood film-set and the pyramidical profusion of balconies, portals and arcuate roof seems merely bizarre, it is in fact one of the buildings of Jaipur most significantly influenced by traditional local styles. The temples of northern India relied heavily on arched and balconied openings to admit light into the *sanctum*, and the Jain temple-builders in particular used the simple device of repeating a single structural *motif* in tier after tier to achieve a strong vertical thrust on their most successful buildings. The eleventh-century Sasbahu temple at nearby Gwalior has three tiers of clustered and stylistically repetitive balcony openings and achieves a visual effect which is remarkably like the Hawa Mahal.

At Jaipur one can see a crucial stage in a process of architectural synthesis which is quite remarkable in its breadth and which takes one from early Hindu and Jain temple styles through to the legacy of Imperial Britain. The Moghuls came with Persian designs but they used Hindu craftsmen, who added their own flourishes. Thus the Moghul style was already a synthesis of Persia and India, and towards the end of the Moghul period the influence of Italian artists also crept into the Moghul style. At Jaipur, Jai Singh II and his successors married this Moghul style to a variety of native brides. There was not only the martial architecture of the Rajput fortress, but also the Jain religious style which comes through most forcefully in the Hawa Mahal, and a Bengali touch too, transmitted through Jai Singh's principal architect, Vidyodhar, who came from that region. The latter shows up most noticeably in the characteristic drooping roofs which supposedly originate from bamboo structures common in Bengal.

But what Jaipur took from the past it also willed to the future. In the nineteenth century Ram Singh hired an English engineer, Sir Swinton Jacob, to build a waterworks. Jacob completed not only this but many other works of civic improvement, and spent most of his working life around the city. In this time he compiled a large portfolio of Indian architectural details and this portfolio has served as a source-book for many later architects. Moreover when in the early twentieth century Edwin Lutyens and his colleagues were preparing the design of the new British Imperial capital at New Delhi they sought around for some examples of Indian architecture to integrate into their basically European conception. One of the places which most impressed them was Jaipur. Although Lutyens was determined that his buildings should express the might of Imperial Britain, and thus should be unmistakably western in design, there are some Rajput-Moghul flourishes in the gateways and roof-top kiosks, and there is lavish use of the reddish sandstone that forms the basis of the 'Pink City'. In architecture and in atmosphere Jaipur is poised between the colourful royal past and the bustling cosmopolitan present.

JAISALMER

The Thar desert is hot, flat and monotonously brown. It seems to earn
its name, which means 'deathly'. The road is apparently going nowhere,
and there is little sign of life. Yet after one hundred and seventy-five
straight miles, when the map shows that you are about to cross over
from 'rare cultivation' to 'positive sterility', an improbable sight looms
up from the expanse of desert. The mirage of a vast, battered ocean-
going liner. You are at Jaisalmer. The middle of nowhere. A huge
fortification at the world's end.

The Rajput princes of Jodhpur, Bikaner and Jaisalmer ruled over the
Thar or Great Indian Desert. *Thar* is a contraction of *marust'hali* or
'abode of death', and this sandy waste, five hundred miles long and
nearly two hundred wide, forms an imposing natural barrier between
the valley of the Indus and the plains of northern India. When the
Marquis of Elphinstone set out across the desert on a mission to Afghanistan in 1808 he found the passage slow and dangerous:

'We came to sand-hills, which at first were covered with bushes, but afterwards
were naked piles of loose sand, rising one after another like the waves of the
sea, and marked on the surface by the wind like drifted snow. There were roads
through them, made solid by the treading of animals; but off the road our
horses sunk into the sand above the knee.'

But there was in fact life in this abode of death. Wherever there was water, Elphinstone found a poor village. Occasionally he came across shepherds with ragged herds of goats. And from time to time he passed majestic lines of loaded camels carrying all manner of produce between the Indus and Afghan marts on one side and the towns of northern and western India on the other. Water, goats and trade provided a foundation on which some fugitive Rajput princes could found kingdoms and build castles on the sand.

Jaisal was already the chief of a nearby fort when in 1156 he discovered the Gadisar lake, and the Trikuta or three-peaked hill which was then the home of a hermit. The hermit, according to legend, invited Jaisal to build a fort. It was an ideal site. The lake was one of the biggest oases in the heart of the desert and the hill was the highest for miles around. Jaisal and his successors threw an enormous wall with 'ninety-nine beetling bastions' around the rocky hill and built inside it a city that was well defended both from the shifting sands of the desert and the assaults of neighbouring tribes. The lake supported an economy of goats and millet, the fortress acted as a secure *caravanserai* for the traders passing from east to west.

The princes of Jaisalmer built a series of palaces, and the itinerant

The Fort at Jaisalmer.

The intricate filigree work in the palace courtyard was carved by Muslim craftsmen for Jaisalmer's Hindu rulers.

A belltower in the palace compound. The drooping roofs, known as Bangladhar because of their resemblance to the thatched roofs of Bengali village huts, became a characteristic feature in Rajput architecture.

merchants built a number of *havelis* or lodges, all in an architecture which is ornate, distinctive and modelled to suit the demands of residence in the desert. The houses climbed up as high as possible to catch the breeze, and the richer *havelis* were surmounted by overhanging cantilevered balconies. The living quarters were constructed out of thick blocks of stone to provide insulation against the sun, and this deliberately heavy architecture merged with the walls and battlements to give a picture of one enormous fortification. But closer inspection reveals a riot of fine detail. The red and yellow sandstones quarried locally were remarkably suited to the stone-mason's art. They were easy to carve into intricate shapes and patterns, and they hardened with weathering over time. Houses were decked out with canopied balconies to protect the inner walls from the rays of the sun, and with the decorative pierced screens known as *jalis*, which hid the women in the seclusion of *purdah*. In the centre of the town there was not just one

palace but three; one for the king, one for his queen, and one for his collection of concubines. The king's palace looks out onto the old city through a mass of carved porticoes, while those of the women present stern, blind walls to the outside world.

Coloured tiles and intricate sandstone carving face the imposing entrance to the Durbar Hall and banqueting room.

All this has been wonderfully preserved because of the isolation of the desert. Until very recently the only access to the city was by camel. Jaisalmer has loitered around the margin of Rajput history and has for the most part avoided the travails of the other Rajput states to the west. The early Muslim king of Delhi, Allauddin Khalji, besieged and sacked the city at the very end of the thirteenth century because the Jaisalmer ruler made an unlucky move in his general policy of pillaging the desert trade to raise revenue: he seized a caravan of fifteen hundred horses and fifteen hundred mules loaded with treasure which was the tribute of the Indus valley on its way to Allauddin's coffers in Delhi. But after some years in exile the princes regained Jaisalmer. They became tributary to the Moghuls but not until late in the seventeenth century, and they were the last of the Rajput princes to make a treaty with the British. In between they fought with the other tribes of the desert, and evolved a history of palace intrigue, treachery, abduction and murder that could only take place in the heat and isolation of such a desert stronghold. By the time the British arrived the ruler had allowed the post of prime minister to become hereditary and now these two royal dynasties were poisoning one another with monotonous regularity.

Whatever the costs of this cloistered history it has left a city, an architecture and a style of life which are relatively undamaged by the modern world. At the end of the nineteenth century, the Maharawal Salivahan of Jaisalmer built a new palace. He placed it outside the old walls of the city partly because the security of British rule had quelled the worst excesses of the desert feuds, and partly because he believed that it was a curse on the old city-palace which was keeping the rate of

LEFT *A* haveli *or merchant's house in Jaisalmer. The elaborate stone screens serve a purpose since* purdah *is still observed here.*

Paniharis or water-carriers pass through the central courtyard of the Mandir Palace on their way to the Gadisar Lake.

Hindu auspicious signs frame the entrance to the private apartments of the Mandir Palace.

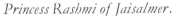
Princess Rashmi of Jaisalmer.

The royal horse and royal camel decked out ceremonially in some of the finest Rajasthani silver-work.

mortality in the ruling family almost up to the level it had attained in the bad old days of warfare and assassination. But this palace is quite unlike many others built at the same period. It is almost entirely untouched by European architectural influences, and barely affected by Moghul ideas. Rather it is firmly Indo-Saracenic – the term for the style which draws on Islamic patterns but which is firmly distinguished from any Muslim architecture built outside India. It is in fact a blend of the Rajput style and of Islamic influences which were carried to Jaisalmer by the camel trains from Afghanistan, Persia and beyond. There are squat pavilions, bulbous domes, green and yellow tiles and fluted pillars in an evidently Muslim style; but equally there is much which is derived from old Jaisalmer itself. The outer walls of the palace look fortified and merge into the walls of the old city. There are *zenana* quarters dark as dungeons which suddenly open out onto courtyards decorated with latticed screens and carved balconies. And there are tiers of balconies pierced with arches of *jali*-work, rimmed with spear-head *motifs* and sheltered by the drooping canopies, all of which are marks of Hindu craftsmanship and are seen here in the purest form.

Her Highness Maharani Mukut
Rajya Laxmi of Jaisalmer.

The Yuvraj, or heir to the Jaisalmer
throne, held by his manservant.

The people too seem preserved from another time, and the Rajput men still dress as Colonel James Tod described them a century and a half ago:

'a *jamah*, or tunic of white cloth or chintz reaching to the knee; the cumurbund, or *ceinture*, tied so high as to present no appearance of waist; trousers very loose, and in many folds, drawn tight at the ankle, and a turban, generally of a scarlet colour, rising conically full a foot from the head'.

The women, children and even the horses are often submerged with jewellery. As Tod again noticed, the women favour 'the *chaori*, rings of ivory or bone, with which they cover their arms from the shoulder to the wrist', while the men sport rings and, occasionally, enormous earrings. The silver jewellery is made throughout Rajasthan by village craftsmen; each village has a distinctive style which is instantly recognisable to the local connoisseur. In the palace the furniture is all of silver, for only that material can imitate the colour of the moon, which is the ancestor of the ruling family. Luckily, some things change slowly, if at all. Medieval India is still in existence in Jaisalmer, and in the isolation of the desert it looks as if it will remain that way.

JODHPUR

For five centuries Jodhpur was the capital of the desert principality of Marwar, where the rains failed every three years and famines were an accepted part of the way of life. But ironically the desert has associated the name of Marwar with wealth and prosperity. Over the centuries the caravans crossed the desert and made Marwar a crossroads and *entrepôt*:

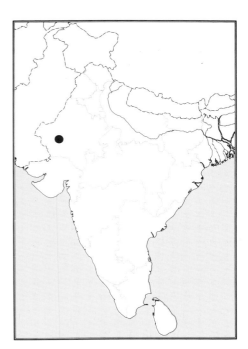

'where the productions of India, Cashmere, and China, were interchanged for those of Europe, Africa, Persia and Arabia. Caravans from the ports of Cutch and Guzerat imported elephants' teeth, copper, dates, gum-arabic, borax, coco-nuts, broadcloths, silks, sandal-wood, camphor, dyes, drugs, oxide and sulphuret of arsenic, spices, coffee etc. In exchange they exported chintzes, dried fruit, *jeeroh*, asafoetida from Mooltan, sugar, opium, silks and fine cloth, potash, shawls, dyed blankets, arms and salt of home manufacture.'

This trade turned the inhabitants of the region of death, the Marwaris, into the richest and most famous bankers in India. The threat of famine and the threat of forced taxation by the local warrior princes drove them out of their homeland and made them famous as financiers and business-men throughout India and later throughout the world.

But Marwar is not only desert and desert traders. The territory runs up to the Aravalli hills and straddles the main route from Delhi to Gujarat; thus Marwar, unlike Jaisalmer, has not been able to avoid the main currents of Rajput and Moghul history. The capital was founded at Jodhpur in 1459, doubtless because of the existence of a steep and

seemingly impregnable rock with an unstinted view over the desert surrounds. The fortress provided the necessary defence against Moghul attack, and enabled the Jodhpur prince to make an honourable treaty with the Moghul Emperor. The Jodhpur rulers helped the Emperor Akbar to conquer Gujarat and the rewards of these expeditions helped to embellish the city. Jodhpur reached the height of its influence at the Moghul court when in the 1580s Rao Udai Singh married his sister to the Emperor Akbar and his daughter to the Moghul heir-apparent. While this alliance is now considered an affront to Rajput honour, at the time it seemed more inconvenient to Akbar than to the Jodhpur princes. While Akbar's Rajput wife, Jodh Bai, became a powerful influence at the Moghul court and persuaded the Emperor to increase the territories and the titles of the Jodhpur house, the Emperor Akbar himself found that he had to bow to his Hindu wife's religious and feminine sensitivity and give up 'beef, garlic, onions and the wearing of a beard'. The Muslim chronicler who recorded these facts, and who clearly disapproved of this compromise with the wishes of the infidel, noted that 'the last three things are inconvenient in kissing'.

But the royal women who remained behind at Jodhpur were not always indulged in quite this way. From time to time the walls of the old palace and city show the imprint of a hand that records the last act of a loyal wife before she burned herself on her husband's pyre. There are even carvings of these hand imprints to honour the act of *suttee*, for

The Umaid Bhawan Palace, designed by H. V. Lanchester and built between 1929 and 1944, has eight dining halls and a private theatre among its 347 rooms.

although Jodhpur has nothing in its history to rival the scale of the *johar* in the fort of Chittore, it still demanded great sacrifice from its royal women. Moreover the royal act of *suttee* was always made more severe because of the number of the prince's consorts. At one dynastic juncture, two queens and seven concubines immolated themselves, while the princely line was only saved because a third queen, seven months pregnant at the time, was forcibly restrained from joining them on the pyre. Upon another royal death, six queens and fifty-eight concubines burnt themselves with the words: 'Without our lord, even life is death.'

For Jodhpur the patronage of the Moghuls brought glory – Akbar called Udai Singh of Jodhpur the 'King of the Desert' – and then ruin. After the reign of Akbar the succession to the Moghul throne was decided not by convention but by conflict, and it was simply impossible for a courtier deeply involved in the affairs of the Moghul dynasty to back the right side in each one of the many dynastic wars. Jaswant Singh of Jodhpur supported the wrong man in the war which finally placed Aurangzeb on the Moghul throne. He was then apparently reconciled with the Emperor but before long was sent off on an imperial expedition to Afghanistan where, mysteriously and probably treacherously, he met his death. Aurangzeb then tried to seize the infant heir to the Jodhpur throne who was in Delhi at the time. The Jodhpur retainers played a desperate game of hide-and-seek with the Imperial Guards in the streets of the city and finally smuggled the baby out to safety hidden in a basket of sweetmeats. After this the women of Jodhpur stranded in Delhi blew themselves up with gunpowder in order that they should not fall into the Emperor's vengeful hands. Later, in the struggle that followed Aurangzeb's death, the Jodhpur prince again supported the weaker party and, at the end of a long Moghul intrigue, was killed by his own son. This act of patricide split the ranks of the royal and noble families in Jodhpur and began a century of civil war and dynastic confusion.

The eighteenth-century Italian traveller, Nicolo Manucci, called the Rajputs 'the most warlike people in all Hindoostan' and thought that 'if they were only united among themselves, they could easily expel the Moghul from Hindoostan'. But they were far from united and spent far more time fighting among themselves than fighting against their various overlords. By the mid-eighteenth century the political morality of Jodhpur had sunk so low that when, amidst the intrigues and murders of these years, a prince was asked where the state of Jodhpur lay, he replied: 'It is here, in the sheath of my dagger.' By the end of the century, the state had been overrun by the Marathas and then by the British.

The resurgence of Jodhpur had to wait until the twentieth century. From the 1870s to the 1920s Jodhpur was dominated by the personality of Pratap Singh. He was not in fact the Maharaja, but a younger son of

The present Maharaja Gaja Singh wearing an emerald necklace from the crown jewels.

the ruling line who three times was called on to act as regent. He became famous for his charming manners, idiosyncratic English, fanatical royalism, and for his tough sportiveness. As one British official recorded:

'A keen soldier, a lover of horse and hound, the intimate friend of three British sovereigns, he was a type that appealed to the Englishman. His devotion to the British Crown was almost a religion . . . He speared leopards single-handed and he thought nothing of flinging himself off his horse on to a wounded boar in thick jungle, putting it on its back and trussing it.'

He travelled to England to meet Queen Victoria in 1885 and was mortified when *en route* he lost all his baggage; the ship sank at Suez while he was ashore, and took with it all his clothes and jewels. It was not the cost which appalled Pratap Singh but the thought that he would have to appear before his royal idol without his usual resplendent apparel. However, some open-handed *largesse* persuaded the Suez dockside urchins to recover some of the jewels, and friends in London

A wall at the entrance to the Jodhpur Fort where the ladies of the royal house left a handprint before committing suttee *on the funeral pyre of their husbands.*

came up with gifts of fine silks and brocades which enabled him to cut a fine figure before his queen.

He liked a hard life. He horrified one of the rather sickly Jodhpur heirs under his care by trying to toughen the boy up with a course in ascetic and athletic living. The poor chap had to sleep on a stone bed and to limber up by wrestling with a barely muzzled panther. But Pratap Singh was also something of a prude. He visited Paris and found it horribly decadent. And he refused an invitation to make the acquaintance of a rather daringly dressed lady at a Viceregal ball with the wonderfully quaint remark: 'I think not very gentlemanly lady.'

Pratap Singh gave Jodhpur a reputation for progressiveness and this was continued by the Maharaja Umaid Singh who was determined that Jodhpur should be a 'model state'. But it was a model state weighed down by its feudal past. When in 1923 the monsoon failed for the third time in succession, the only manner in which the young Umaid Singh could think of providing employment for his starving population was to put them to work in building a palace.

It was a work of extraordinary folly. For astrological reasons he decided to place the palace, Umaid Bhavan, on the Chittar Hill, even though this created untold difficulties over the water supply – no small concern in a virtually desert tract. It also required a small army of donkeys to carry over half a million loads of earth to the top of the hill to create a base for the palace, and the construction of twelve miles of railway to bring the cream-pink sandstone from the nearest quarry.

Then the Maharaja chose H. V. Lanchester to serve as the architect. Lanchester was already famous in Britain for a style of heavy, self-important civic architecture. He counted among his monuments town halls in Cardiff and Deptford, a university at Leeds, hospitals in London and Birmingham, and the Wesleyan Central Hall at Westminster. He had already begun on a career as a town planner and it was this that had taken him to India in the first place. Umaid Bhavan was his only excursion into stately architecture and it clearly carries the imprint of Lanchester's civic training.

For Lanchester was unwilling to dabble too deeply in Indian architectural styles. The layout repeated the traditional divisions of an Indian palace, but here these divisions were translated into wings as in a hospital or town hall – the reception rooms at the centre, the staff quarters to the left, and the *zenana* to the right. On matters of detail, Lanchester was quite firm:

'In the architectural treatment and ornamental detail, any use of "Indo-Saracenic" features was regarded as inappropriate, in view of the fact that the States of Rajasthan only came to a very limited extent under Muslim domination.'

Thus while the outside was, but for a few indigenous flourishes, civic-monolithic, the interior contained a confusion of Renaissance mimicry. It possessed three hundred and forty-seven rooms, including eight dining rooms and a banqueting hall for three hundred people. The domed central hall rose to one hundred and ninety feet, and deep in the basement nestled a swimming pool. There were suites for princes and commoners, English and Indian kitchens, a ballroom, a theatre for stage and cinema, and air-conditioning throughout. There was a profusion of goldwork and stacks of imported furniture, while even the murals of traditional Indian subjects were painted by modern European artists. Outside was an immaculate copy of an eighteenth-century garden.

It took fifteen years to complete. Today there are neither lawns nor flowers but the peacocks still strut among the empty pools. Umaid Bhavan remains an example of feudal illogicality – a palace that was built as a measure of famine relief.

BIKANER

Desert kings should have remote and exotic capitals where the architecture owes little to 'progress' or 'civilisation' and where the camel seems much more at home than the motor car. Bikaner does not disappoint. The Lallgarh palace of the rulers of Bikaner rises up in a mass of turrets, ramparts and kiosks in a yellow, arid and treeless landscape. Bikaner has had a warlike past – it was nearer to Delhi than the other Rajput desert principalities of Jaisalmer and Jodhpur and thus spent much more time fighting the Muslim invaders – and it is right that this striking building interposed between the massive expanses of sand and sky should look at first glance like a pure example of Rajput martial architecture. The squat, solid-looking mass of pink sandstone is covered in battlements and bastions, the gateway is square and strong, the walls are high and handsome.

But a second glance reveals several disturbing details. The battlements have a rather delicate look; the kiosks over the bastions possess a rather fragile grace. The walls are smothered with windows, which would be a careless addition to a truly defensive building, and the horizontal lines of the windows and battlements are somehow too well proportioned and

regular. And finally the palace is in fact *outside* the sturdy walls that ring *Lallgarh.*
the city. This was clearly not a military building. Indeed it was built,
not in the fifteenth and sixteenth centuries when Bikaner was fighting
off Muslim raids, nor even in the seventeenth when the ruler of Bikaner
carried the Moghul standard to the south of India, but in the very early
years of this century when Bikaner was emerging as one of the British
rulers' favourite examples of a 'Native State'.

The domain of Bikaner was founded in the fifteenth century after
Bika, a scion of the Jodhpur house, had set out with three hundred
followers to conquer the deserts to the north. In the period before the
Moghuls hemmed the Rajputs in, such forays were quite common and
usually successful, for the invaders careered off 'with a determination to
slay or be slain' on carefully chosen auspicious days 'when the warlike
creed of the Rajpoots made the abstraction of territory from foe or
friend a matter of religious duty'. The pastoral desert tribes, already
riven by their own petty feuds, were little match for this ferocity.

The subsequent history is rather more tawdry. There was the usual
alliance with the Moghuls, a debilitating centuries-long feud with

LEFT *A member of the Bikaner Camel Corps stands in the main porch of Lallgarh.*

The carving on the red-sandstone walls of Bikaner is like a reference catalogue of Rajput art.

A cloister of peacock arches rings a courtyard in Laxmi Vilas, the section of the palace which houses the guest rooms.

The filigree work on the upper storeys is carved from marble. Maharaja Ganga Singh loved the coolness of this elaborate octagonal room at the front of the palace.

RIGHT *A marble bust of Queen Victoria in the entrance hall of Lallgarh.*

Jodhpur, and some spectacular succession disputes. Guj Singh started off the best of these by leaving, at his death in 1787, a total of sixty-one sons; only six could claim legitimacy and thus a right to the throne, but this was quite enough. The civil war finally fizzled out when the combatants began to miss their creature comforts. Like many Rajput princes, those at Bikaner liked nothing quite so much as to smoke opium and sip the liqueur made from gold, silver, ashes of pearls and the brains of sheep and goats; it was known as *asha*, reserved strictly for the consumption of the royal houses, and famed as an aphrodisiac. By the time the British arrived on the scene Bikaner was hard-pressed by rival neighbours and rebellious subjects.

Three things rescued Bikaner from this sorry state of decline – camels, a railway, and sand-grouse.

Bikaner's great military asset was its camels. Throughout the nineteenth century, while the British were trying to settle the North West

The Shiv Vilas banqueting hall seats
four hundred. The inmates of the
Bikaner jail made the Persian-style
carpet in the 1920s.

The marble-floored corridor running
from the state rooms to the royal
apartments is decorated with trophies
of the chase, fading photographs of
hunting parties and a collection of
Animalier bronzes.

Frontier, the camel was their principal means of military transport, and in the twentieth century the British Army again found it needed camels to settle its European wars. Ratan Singh of Bikaner presented the British with two hundred camels to assist them in the Afghan war of 1842, and started a relationship which would gradually bring Bikaner favour and political importance. During the Great Mutiny Bikaner sheltered many European men and women, and was duly rewarded with an addition of territory. Then Ganga Singh succeeded to the throne in 1898 and organised the Bikaner Camel Corps, which soon gained a reputation as the most flamboyant military unit of modern times.

As Ganga Singh was aware, his camels might act as a perfectly good calling-card at Viceregal House, but they could hardly serve as the basis for a lasting romance. After all, the Imperial Gazetteer of India had just concluded that 'the people of Bikaner are exceedingly dirty both in their persons and habits' and that no other town in the vicinity could 'vie with Bikaner as regards the grotesque irregularity of its thorough-fares'. Camels were not the right means to dispel the idea that Bikaner was a grubby feudal backwater. Ganga Singh decided to acquire some-thing which was much more likely to touch the Anglo-Saxon heart. He built a railway.

He also promoted a coal-mining industry at the end of his desert railway, and within ten years he had trebled the state's income and turned much of the revenue into the sort of public buildings which spelled progress. Ganga Singh's final coup was the sand-grouse. They were hardly his invention since they arrived every year on their October migration. But this was also the season when the heat eased, the 'cold weather' began, and the tired, 'sun-dried' officials of British India recovered enough of their energies to think about recreation. Ganga Singh soon realised the diplomatic potential of his yearly flying visitors.

They were not ordinary sand-grouse. They were of the variety known, appropriately, as the 'Imperial sand-grouse', and were reckoned by some gourmets to be the tastiest game-bird in the world. Ganga Singh made them the centre-piece of a great Imperial social occasion. Itiner-aries of visiting monarchs were often re-scheduled to fit in the Bikaner sand-grouse shoot, and Viceroys would put aside the business of Empire in order to attend. However, the sand-grouse lasted barely three hours, so Ganga Singh appended a chase after bustard and black buck (often conducted from a Rolls-Royce), a miniature military tattoo performed by a company of camel-riders in hoods and black chainmail, and a memorable banquet. Ganga Singh had the sand-grouse shoot in good working order before the Prince of Wales's visit in 1905.

The combination of military assistance, industrial enlightenment and bloodsports ensured that Ganga Singh would be styled an 'Ideal Prince'. He was invited to sign the Treaty of Versailles on behalf of his country, and he emerged as a powerful figure in the political organi-

sation of Indian princes which the British conjured up as a counter-weight to nationalism in the aftermath of the First World War.

He also channelled the profits of his mines and railways into the construction of the palace of Lallgarh. For the design he drew on the services of Sir Samuel Swinton Jacob, an Indian Army officer from an established Indian Army family, who had become one of the greatest living experts on Indian architecture and particularly on the Rajput style. He designed many public buildings throughout India, including the Secretariat offices at the summer capital of Simla, St Stephen's College in Delhi, the Bank (now State Bank) of Madras and the Victoria Memorial Hall at Peshawar. He was a leading figure in the attempt to blend indigenous Indian designs with the demands of modern living and most of his work has a curiously hybrid look. But on Rajput architecture Jacob became something of a dogmatist. While at Jaipur, he had compiled and published an enormous portfolio of architectural details and this portfolio served as a source-book for many other modern architects, both European and Indian. In the Bikaner palace, and in several other buildings he built for princely patrons around Rajputana, he turned this academic study of Rajput architectural detail into solid form.

In the classic manner of a Rajput fort, Bikaner's Lallgarh has very little decoration on the outside except for the crowning glory of battlements and umbrella-type cupolas. In a similarly classic manner, the interior is arranged around two spacious courtyards. Moreover here the decorative detail owes little to Moghul influences and much more to Rajput styles which predate the Moghul invasions. There is little of the Moghul inlay and mirror-work; the emphasis instead is on a profusion of hand-carved friezes, pillars and delicate *jali* screens. The designs have been taken from the cluster of palaces in the old Bikaner fort and filtered through Jacob's keen academic knowledge. However, Jacob's European background, and his patron's modern aspirations, make sudden inroads into the design. The strong horizontal lines of the battlements and serried ranks of windows on the exterior owe much to the Renaissance styles so popular in nineteenth and early twentieth century Europe; the interior has refined Italianate colonnades, drawing rooms worthy of a European hunting-lodge, and a banqueting hall to seat four hundred; and outside vividly green lawns have been wrested away from the desert to create an ordered and restful garden. But despite these touches, it is still an unmistakable piece of work – one of the purest essays in Rajput martial architecture which was, ironically, built by a British army officer on the profits of a railway.

RIGHT *The first inner courtyard of Lallgarh.*

58

BUNDI

'The *coup d'oeil* of the castellated palace of Boondi, from whichever side you approach it, is perhaps the most striking in India; but it would require a drawing on an extremely large scale to comprehend either its picturesque beauties or its grandeur; . . . for it is an aggregate of palaces, each having the name of its founder; and yet the whole so well harmonises, and the character of the architecture is so uniform, that its breaks or fantasies appear only to rise from the peculiarity of the position, and serve to diversify its beauties.'

Thus Lieutenant-Colonel James Tod recorded in his diary on September 13 1820. Nor could Tod's opinion be described as amateur. He had been appointed by the East India Company as political agent in Rajasthan; he had by the time of this diary entry seen almost all the forts and palaces of the leading Rajput houses; he was soon to emerge as the exuberant historian of the Rajputs and to present the world with twelve hundred pages of the *Annals and Antiquities of Rajast'han*, which is still being regularly reprinted. Among the palaces of Rajasthan, Tod allotted Bundi 'the first rank'.

Bundi's glories were well defended. The state is buried deep in the centre of Rajasthan amidst a range of rough hills which are crossed by only four passes and which have always been Bundi's first line of defence. The second line is the jumble of rocks, rising steeply from the valley of the river Chambal and providing the foundation for the town and the backdrop for the extraordinary view that so impressed Colonel Tod. Finally there are the walls themselves, which climb up and down the rocky slope in a chaos of planes and angles, and creep along the crest of the hills like a great brown crocodile.

LEFT *The Chatar Mahal, built in the mid-seventeenth century, clambers up the hillside above Bundi town.*

Such splendid defences divided Bundi from the main currents of Rajput history and from the forces of change. The Moghuls paid little attention to this out-of-the-way region. A band of Pathans who were brought in to guard the palace in the sixteenth century found it such a pleasant change from the constant warring of Afghanistan that their descendants still live in Bundi and guard the palace. Until a very late date, the Bundi armies still fought on a pattern which had once been terrifyingly effective but had long been outmoded by superior weaponry: the Bundi troops collected into a tight phalanx known as the *gole* and then this ball of men, bristling with spears and sabres, charged the enemy like a demented porcupine. By the turn of the eighteenth century the greater use of guns and horses had made the *gole* a sadly expensive military formation and in two battles fought on behalf of the Moghuls the Bundi forces lost twelve princes of the royal line and the head of every single clan.

Bundi fell under the British yoke in 1818, but seems to have survived the nineteenth century innocent of the blessings of British rule. When in 1911 Maharaja Raghubir Singh of Bundi was treated by a western doctor for a serious illness, it caused 'quite a sensation and provoked a great deal of public comment'.

The Chatar Mahal seen from the Taragarh fort above. The palace seems to grow out of the hillside and possibly into it too; there are said to be secret chambers built into the heart of the hills.

Most of Bundi's history is thus a rather private history, and much of it concerns the attempts to protect that privacy. The Moghul, Maratha and British overlords were less troublesome interlopers than Bundi's Rajput neighbours and some of the state's ambitious inhabitants. The state was carved out of territory which was originally claimed by the princes of Chittore (Udaipur) and their successors were always anxious to make Bundi dependent and tributary. Moreover as Amber (Jaipur) rose to the front rank of Rajput states under the umbrella of Moghul patronage, their princes also were anxious to absorb the hilly fastness of Bundi. Thus the two great warriors of Bundi's past, Chatar Sal and Umed Singh, fought not only against Moghul armies, but also against overbearing neighbours and homegrown upstarts.

Chatar Sal was the hero of fifty-two combats. He had served the Emperor Shah Jahan so loyally that he refused to make a diplomatic transfer of his allegiance to Shah Jahan's son and usurper, Aurangzeb, and died fighting against Aurangzeb's army. He built the largest and most remarkable of the palaces jumbled together in the avalanche of stonework that runs down the hillside at Bundi. In keeping with Bundi's tradition of backward parochialism, the building bore little resemblance to other Rajput palaces built at the same period. Despite Chatar Sal's involvement in Moghul affairs, any Moghul influence over the design of his palace was kept firmly in check. The material used was not the red or yellow sandstones favoured by the Moghul craftsmen, but the greenish serpentine from the state's own quarries. The decoration

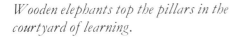
Wooden elephants top the pillars in the courtyard of learning.

The architecture of the Chatar Mahal is some of the most traditional to be found among all the Rajput palaces.

avoided the columns and arches that distinguished the Moghul style, and stuck to a purer form of Rajput design. The characteristics of this style were the drooping, arcuate roofs; the lotus flowers on the spandrels of the entrances; the use of the elephant as a decorative symbol; the avoidance, as far as possible, of the construction of a true arch; and the proliferation of richly ornamented brackets to hold up balconies, to surmount pillars and hold up the roof, and to elaborate a false arch in an otherwise square gateway. The local stone did not allow the builders to add the delicately carved *jali* screens which were the other mark of Rajput style, and the builders could scarcely resist endowing the interior with some of the lavish ornamentation of Moghul origin, but Chatar Mahal was very distinctively a Rajput building. The high terraces of the building served as the ruler's public reception rooms with a breathtaking view down over the crazed geometry of terraces and gardens of the other palaces, and across to the valley of the Chambal river and the hills beyond. 'Whoever has seen the palace of Boondi,' wrote Tod after he had been received on this terrace, 'can easily picture to himself the hanging-gardens of Semiramis.'

In the early eighteenth century the ruler of Jaipur made a treacherous pact with the guard of the Bundi citadel, and turned the princes out of their capital. Thus Umed Singh was born in exile in 1731, and at the age of thirteen he began his campaign to regain his patrimony. He succeeded in taking Bundi, lost it again almost immediately, and then only made sure of success on the second attempt by enlisting the help of the Maratha adventurer, Malhar Rao Holkar, the founder of Indore. This was an expensive alliance, since the Holkar demanded a reward in territory, and the Bundi that Umed Singh regained was, in his own words, 'a heap of cotton'.

But Umed Singh then put aside the sword and in the next eighteen years made his 'heap of cotton' secure and prosperous. He gained

recognition as a patron of the arts and ensured that among the many
schools of Rajasthani painting of the eighteenth century there would be
a 'Bundi school'. Some of the best examples still line the walls of the
Chitra Shala or Art Gallery – illustrations of religious and mythical
stories, hunting scenes, and events from Bundi's history.

Yet in this period Umed Singh committed one singularly violent act.
He sought out the old retainer who had delivered Bundi fort into the
hands of Jaipur and murdered him along with his son and grandson.
Some years later he regretted the crime, and as an act of penance he
abdicated in favour of his son and set off on a pilgrimage. Before his
departure in 1771, the state performed a mock ritual of his funeral. A
dummy of Umed Singh was placed on a funeral pyre, his son had his
head shaved in the traditional act of filial mourning, and the population
indulged in twelve days of ritual lamentation. Umed Singh set off to a
mountain retreat to prepare himself, and then traversed the length and
breadth of India. Though a pilgrim, he was still a Rajput and he was
still appreciative of the power of his enemies. He did not sport the
usual saffron robe, staff and begging bowl of the ascetic, but took as
much of his armour and weaponry as he could carry:

'He wore a quilted tunic,' reports Colonel Tod, 'which would resist a sabre-cut;
besides a matchlock, a lance, a sword, a dagger, and their appurtenances of
knives, pouches and priming horn; he had a battle-axe, a javelin, a tomahawk,
a discus, bow and quiver of arrows; and it is affirmed that such was his mus-
cular power, even when threescore and ten years had blanched his beard in

wandering to and fro thus accoutred, that he could place the whole of his panoply within his shield, and with one arm not only raise it, but hold it for some seconds extended.'

To the very end, Bundi responded slowly to the outside world. 'The administration,' noted one British official visitor in the early twentieth century, 'is inclined to be primitive.' Indeed, the palace still spurns centuries of technology and keeps time with a crude water clock; a bowl fills with water each hour and an attendant records the time by beating a gong.

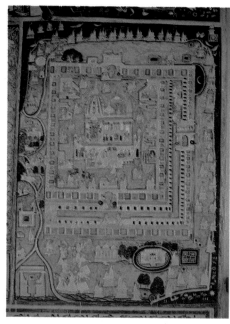

LEFT The *Chitra Shala* or 'painted hall' commissioned by Umed Singh and carried out between 1750 and 1770. The paintings depict religious stories as well as romantic and military incidents in the history of the Bundi royal family.

Finally Maharaja Bahadur Singh fell in with the other princes under the Raj, and built a new palace, on the foundations of an old hunting-lodge. This Phoolsagar palace had the guest apartments, ballroom and shooting facilities which the visiting British dignitaries so appreciated. But the work was not started until 1945, two years before the British left, and the palace is still not quite finished. Bundi is deliciously behind the times.

Phoolsagar, the Maharaja's hunting-lodge, is built around a cooling lake.

KOTAH

Peering out from the terraces of the Bundi palace in September 1820, Colonel Tod reckoned he could make out the city of Kotah some forty miles away across the river Chambal. He had already visited Kotah and could not help noting the vast difference in the atmosphere of the capitals of these sister principalities. Bundi seemed remote, charming, pickled in medieval vinegar; Kotah, on the other hand:

'is very imposing, and impresses the mind with a more lively notion of wealth and activity than most cities in India . . . The scene is crowded with objects animate and inanimate. Between the river and the city are masses of people plying various trades'.

The contrast remains today. While Bundi remains sleepy and picturesque, Kotah is the fastest growing industrial city in the state of Rajasthan, has quintupled its population in a century, and sports tall factory chimneys amidst endless rows of uniformly squalid labour colonies.

The reason for the contrast is not hard to find. While Bundi stands to one side at the edge of the hills, Kotah sits firmly on the valley floor and straddles one of the main routes crossing central India from the plain of Delhi to the rich lowlands of Gujarat. Once the camel trains and armies passed this way, and now the Delhi-Bombay railway runs through. While Bundi's history has a private flavour, Kotah has had to deal more efficiently with the outside world. While the hero of eighteenth-century Bundi was a vagabond prince who regained his princedom and then became a hermit, Kotah's equivalent is a statesman and diplomat known variously as the 'Machiavel of Rajwarra' or the 'Talleyrand of north

The murals flanking the 'elephant gate' to the Kotah City Palace show a royal wedding procession.

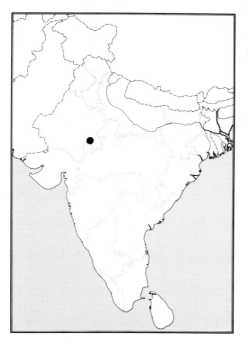

Mirror-work, ebony, ivory and elephants' teeth inlaid on the doors to the Durbar Hall.

India' on account of the role he played in the frantic years of treaties, battles, alliances and feuds on the eve of British rule.

Kotah's territory was once part of Bundi State, but was separated in 1579 by a ruler of Bundi who wished to found a patrimony for a favoured younger son. The rulers of Kotah inherited Bundi's quarrels with the rulers of Chittore (Udaipur) and Amber (Jaipur), and also found it more difficult than their Bundi cousins to avoid the attentions of Moghuls and Marathas. Thus the history of Kotah alternated between periods of expansion under the patronage of indulgent overlords and periods of contraction when the overlords turned nasty. Kotah rulers became masters at the art of diplomacy, for only by astute juggling could the rulers of such a small and vulnerable state keep all their potential enemies at bay. But through the eighteenth century the politics of north India became more complex and more bloody, and survival became even more difficult. It was impossible to choose the right side in *every* Moghul

succession dispute, impossible to guess the intentions of Amber, Mewar or even neighbouring Bundi, and impossible to predict the paths which the armies of marauding Marathas would pursue. Kotah lost almost its entire royal family in a battle that attended Aurangzeb's succession to the Moghul throne, and by 1749 found that the only way to forestall submission to the hated princes of Amber was to accept the supremacy of a Maratha general.

Through these years the rulers of Kotah built their city-palace. The building was hardly designed, but grew when the family prospered, stagnated while the family retreated, and then grew again when fortunes revived. It thus conformed to the pattern which the historian of Indian architecture, Percy Brown, saw as the hallmark of the Rajput seats of power:

'In the interior arrangements of such palaces there are few signs of any ordered plan beyond the inclusion of a large Durbar hall, and a court of assembly, the

The walls and lamp-niches of the Durbar Hall are covered with Rajput miniatures depicting Kotah's history and religious legends.

75

remaining space being occupied by a labyrinth of apartments connected by passages, the whole often dimly lit and steeped in that atmosphere of seclusion and mystery which pervaded the palace life of the time.'

Umed Bhawan, designed by Swinton Jacob at the turn of this century, is set in one of the finest of the palace gardens.

The vulnerability of Kotah meant that the exterior bristled with high walls, strong bastions and fierce ramparts. But there is also much delicate stonework, several fluted domes, and some fine elephant-shaped brackets to support carved balustrades. Tod noted that the cupolas and minarets of the palace gave it 'an air of light elegance'. The close association of Kotah with the politics of Moghul India has endowed the interior with all the grace and decorative intricacy of Moghul design. There is some of the finest black-and-white inlay work, executed with ebony and ivory. There are also rooms packed with Rajput miniatures, plaster mouldings, sandstone carvings, dainty lamp-niches and sparkling mirror-work. The result is a restless, teeming interior which is an appropriate reflection of Kotah's lively history.

Kotah's great diplomat was not a member of the princely family. Zalim Singh descended from a family of Rajputs who had migrated from Kathiawar in the late seventeenth century and become hereditary military commanders for the Kotah princes. Zalim Singh himself got off to a bad start by competing with the Kotah prince for the favours of a lady; and this little indiscretion pushed him into exile. But Zalim Singh soon returned, proved by his military prowess that he was the only man to protect Kotah from the incursions of Amber and the Marathas, and was restored to favour. Before long the prince had died from an illness and Zalim Singh had become Regent of Kotah. The next few years were spent controlling the risings and assassination attempts of the nobles who were jealous of the upstart Zalim Singh and who recognised that a minority was always a good time to try to usurp the throne. There were eighteen plots against his life, including one in which he was lured into the *zenana* and set upon by a group of armed women.

He then set about improving the army by establishing strong castles, adopting European arms and ideas of discipline, and appointing new generals on the grounds of merit rather than birth. To pay for this expensive force he reorganised the revenue system and seized the dues which the headmen and revenue farmers normally stuffed into their own pockets. He also imported new ploughs, dug grain pits and made a dramatic increase in his revenues by working monopolies on the export of grain and opium. On top of that he taxed everything in sight including widows, brooms and gourds. He then entered into diplomatic relations with every military force in the country – the Rajput armies of Jaipur and Udaipur, the Maratha leader Holkar of Indore, the freebooter Amir Khan, the chiefs of the disorderly Pindari robberbands, and finally the British. He befriended many men of power by allowing them sanctuary in Kotah while they were temporarily brought low by the kaleidoscopic fortunes of this chaotic period, and he astutely managed to keep all of Kotah's enemies at loggerheads with one another and thus out of Kotah's territory. In the last act of the drama in 1817-18 Zalim Singh made Kotah the first of the Rajput principalities to accede to the British – with of course the stipulation that the British should recognise his position as Regent and agree to make it hereditary.

But once peace was established Zalim Singh's career quickly declined. The prince of Kotah resented his evident aspiration to found his own dynasty, the people disliked his taxes, the nobles disliked his prominence. Once Zalim Singh's talents were no longer necessary to preserve the independence of Kotah, his dominance became overbearing, distasteful, and unnecessary. The state which had survived the storms of the turn of the century so efficiently, reached the calmer waters of *Pax Britannica* and promptly dissolved in civil war. The British backed the talented

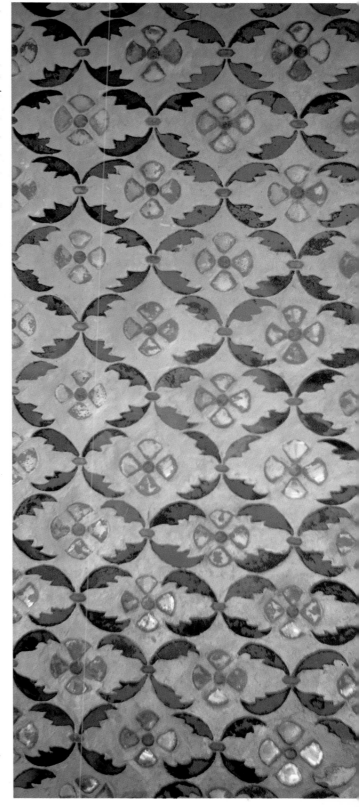

*Every available space on the walls and
ceilings of the City Palace is decorated
with mirror-work in bright colours
and restless patterns.*

Zalim Singh against the Maharaja, but were eventually obliged to still
the quarrel by separating a small principality for Zalim Singh's successors to prevent the feud being passed down to future generations. This
turned out to be a poor expedient. The Kotah ruler, still annoyed that
the British had backed Zalim Singh in their quarrels of the 1820s,
stood aside and let his troops rebel in 1857. Meanwhile, Zalim Singh's
successors made a terrible hash of their little principality. British
political agents spent much of the nineteenth century unseating rulers in
Kotah, and not until 1894 did things settle down, the ruler find his way
back to the throne and the territories become reunited.

Ten years later, Umed Singh II of Kotah celebrated his security with
the erection of a new palace. The architect was Sir Swinton Jacob, who
had spent much of his life in the service of the old enemy of Kotah at
Jaipur, and who also built the palace at Bikaner. His Kotah palace is
more restrained than the *tour de force* at Bikaner. There are still masses of

authentic Rajput architectural details, but the overall design is sedately European. There is an Edwardian drawing room, a banqueting hall crammed with trophies of the chase, a billiard room, tennis courts, eight guest suites, and a garden with some of the most famous herbaceous borders in India.

Umed Singh II also, in his own way, continued Kotah's reputation for careful diplomacy. Many of the native states under British rule had difficulty both with their British overlords and with their noble underlings, but Umed Singh found his own way to deal with this. As Arthur Lothian, a British official who spent most of his life dealing with the Indian states, noted in 1939: 'He was one of the most kind-hearted and simple of men. His custom was every evening to visit the Club and play rummy, with his nobles and officials all round him like a happy family party.'

A wing of the City Palace. The parapets, balustrades, arches and elephant brackets are hallmarks of Rajput architecture.

BHARATPUR

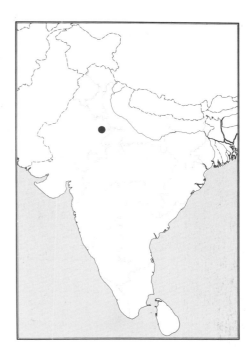

Bharatpur was the only state of any size ruled by a Jat. Over much of northern India the Jats were the people of the land, the backbone of the agricultural population. They had been settled in the area long before Rajput and Maratha had come as conquering princes, and while some Jat chieftains made marriage alliances with these new overlords, most were driven back into the ranks of the peasantry. However they retained a reputation for rebelliousness: they harassed the armies of the Muslim invaders, frequently rose in revolt against the Rajput princes, and in the Punjab they joined the ranks of the Sikh religion and filled the armies which drove the Moghuls out of the north-east. In the late seventeenth century, a Jat village headman called Churaman in the depths of central India banded his fellow Jats together and took advantage of the Moghuls' embroilment with the growing Maratha power. They began to raid through the surrounding countryside until in 1721 the Moghul governor retaliated, dispersed the Jat bands, destroyed their stronghold and had it 'ploughed over by asses'. But the Jat farmers had tasted the heady rewards of freebooting and they soon regrouped under the leadership of Churaman's nephew, Badan Singh. By 1752 they controlled a swathe of territory between Delhi and Agra and the Moghul Emperor was obliged to make Badan Singh a hereditary Raja.

Plunder had brought Badan Singh such rich rewards that he could litter his territory with forts, palaces, parks, country retreats and shooting-lodges. He founded the town of Bharatpur and started building the fort which would later defy two British armies. Suraj Mall inherited these forts, pleasure-houses and the strong Jat army, and had the sense to do absolutely nothing at the critical moment in the eighteenth century. In 1761 the Marathas and Afghans fought one another for the corpse of the Moghul Empire. The battle effectively crippled all the participants. The Afghans, though victorious, went straight back home; the Marathas limped back to central India; the Great Moghul tottered on as an ineffectual puppet; and the lesser chieftains who had become involved were sent back to their fortresses with their tails between their legs. Suraj Mall sat in his resplendent palace until the dust had settled, and then sallied out to pick over the remains. Agra, the premier fort of northern India and home of the Taj Mahal, fell to Jat forces with little resistance, and from there the Jats surged up onto the plain of Delhi. In 1763 Suraj Mall was checked and slain on the field of battle near Agra.

That was the zenith. Succession disputes, Maratha raids and East India Company diplomacy subsequently whittled down Bharatpur territory. Even so in the battles which preceded the final confirmation of British power in central India in 1818, the fort of Bharatpur had a role to play. The Raja of Bharatpur found that he was squeezed between two unwelcome masters – the Company and the Marathas – and tried to switch his loyalties so adeptly that he might retain the semblance of independence. In 1803 he was on the British side, but in 1805 he reneged

OPPOSITE *The entrance porch of the Moti Mahal palace. A red carpet covered the steps when the Maharaja*

81

and threw in his lot with the Maratha Holkar of Indore. Lord Lake, the Company General, was not at all pleased: 'The Bhurtpore Rajah has behaved like a villain', he wrote, 'and deserves chastisement; a very short time would take his forts.' But Lake's anger obscured his judgment. The fort of Bharatpur was exceptionally strong and well-moated. Until then, Lake had been the most successful British general in the Maratha wars but he threw his men carelessly, expensively and uselessly against the walls of the Bharatpur fort. This one action blasted him out of the headlines and into the footnotes of British Imperial history and paved the way for Arthur Wellesley, the future Duke of Wellington.

Shortly after this, however, Bharatpur made a treaty with the British; and the Raja died. His successor, Randhir Singh, could not cope with the demands of warfare and diplomacy in these crucial final years of Indian independence. As we are told in a doctoral thesis from the University of Rajasthan: 'Raja Randhir Singh, a patient of constipation and accustomed to spend more than three hours in the latrine, did not forget the work of administration and allowed his people to report their urgent matters to him even there.' He was just, but he was not very mobile, and he could not take advantage of the decay of Maratha power as his forbears had managed to exploit Moghul decline. The state of Bharatpur remained a thin, watery sliver of territory almost squeezed out of the mass of princely central India by the twin powers of Maratha and Rajput princedoms.

Yet however small, Bharatpur was immensely important for the whole history of princely India under British rule. In 1825 the Bharatpur ruler died and a truculent cousin marched in, displaced the rightful infant heir, and proclaimed himself ruler. By the treaties made in the past two decades the British had undertaken to secure and defend the Bharatpur ruler just as much as any other prince. In fulfilment of this treaty, a Company army marched up and again laid siege to

Standards of war. The gold-plated fish and bird were carried into battle by the Bharatpur army in the eighteenth century.

Bharatpur. The fort again proved stronger than expected and held out for over a month, which gave time for the question of the Company's political obligations towards Bharatpur to mature into a problem of much wider political importance.

In order to justify the invasion of Bharatpur, a leading official of the Company prepared a document in which he argued that the British were now the *paramount* power in India and thus had the 'duty as supreme guardians of general tranquillity, law, and right, to maintain the legal succession'. It was an important assertion for it was the first time the British had defined the claim of absolute supremacy over the princes. Back in London, the Directors of the East India Company disliked this drastic interpretation of British power in the sub-continent, but by the time their opinion could be heard in India, the fort of Bharatpur had fallen, eight thousand soldiers had died in the action, and this carnage had effectively decided the constitutional dispute between the Company Directors and their subordinates. The Company had decisively interfered to uphold the succession in a princely house and all the native rulers of India had heard the mines which breached the walls of Bharatpur for a second time. From now on the princes could not really pretend to be independent, and from now on the British political agents would find themselves embroiled in all the backstairs intrigue, genealogical juggling and venomous ambition which marked so many successions in the princely houses. Moreover the doctrine of paramountcy, laid down during the second siege of Bharatpur, became an acute embarrassment for the British when they finally decided to quit India; for what then became of their obligations to guarantee the princely houses?

But that was far in the future. Under British rule, Bharatpur's watery expanses were famed as a premier shooting ground. There were tiger and black buck, but most of all there were game-birds of all descriptions. The Bharatpur duck shoot was so popular that the Maharaja ordained there should be no more than a hundred guns, and this restriction immediately made the shoot an event on the social calendar and gave the invitation a great social *cachet*. One British official recorded: 'One after another in due succession all the great proconsuls had taken their stand on the famous "Viceroy *bund*" [bank] from which those of them who could shoot straight had counted their victims in hundreds.'

RIGHT *Moti Mahal palace from the garden.*

Bharatpur is surrounded by lakes which once served as the site of the famous Bharatpur duck-shoot and now contain the Keoladeo Ghana bird sanctuary.

After killing an unbelievable number of wild duck (the record bag was 4,273 in a single day) the guests were treated to a champagne breakfast in the marble halls of the old palace.

Elaborate stonework on the upper reaches of Moti Mahal.

Meanwhile, soon after the turn of this century, during the minority of Maharaja Kishen Singh, Bharatpur had acquired a new palace. Moti Mahal was built of local sandstone and combined the traditional with the modern without any embarrassment at all. Open pavilions, lotus arches and Moghul gardens were copied wholesale from the earlier palaces in the Bharatpur Raja's fortress of Deeg. But the profusion of brackets, balconies, canopies and *jali* screens reached back to an earlier Rajput tradition, for although the Bharatpur ruling family were Jats, their customs, their life-style and their pretensions were now much more in line with their Rajput princely neighbours than with those of the ordinary Jat peasant. This warlike and glorious past was recorded in some of the palace's most remarkable ornaments – solid gold images of fish and birds which had been mounted on tall poles and carried into battle by the Jat troops. Finally there were western-style rooms, which the workmen had constructed from pictures in books, and a new wing added on to accommodate the Maharaja's five daughters. Here the usual delicate *jali* work has been curiously but effectively transformed into *art nouveau* designs.

The palace was strewn with emblems of the hunting which represented the Maharaja's last connection with his freewheeling past and which marked out his current role in the social round of British India. The carpet in the library was made of tiger-skins, and the dining room chairs were covered with deer-skins. In the 1940s, however, Maharaja Brijendra Singh became interested in the preservation rather than the slaughter of animals. He patiently befriended the wild *sambhar* (deer) and one British visitor recorded he saw: 'a stag on its hind legs towering above him (the Maharaja) and the little man stretching up on tip-toe to feed it'. Brijendra Singh also gave up some of the site of the famous duck-shoot to serve as a bird-sanctuary and now at Keoladeo Ghana, almost within sight of the Bharatpur palace, the visitor can see Painted storks, Imperial eagles, Dalmatian pelicans, Siberian cranes and a host of other species which are no longer threatened by Viceregal guns.

A marble window in the style of art nouveau.

ALWAR

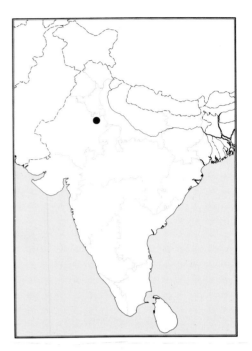

The line of hills which forms the spine of Rajasthan begins with the Aravalli range on the borders of Gujarat and finally tumbles down through the state of Alwar onto the plains of Delhi. Alwar is the last gasp of Rajasthan before it is swallowed up in the hot flat expanse of the north Indian plain. Alwar too was one of the last Rajput states to emerge, and the fortified town founded in 1776 seems to cling to the craggy outcrops of the hills just as desperately as the state of Alwar clung to life.

The family stretches back to a minor offshoot of Jaipur and until the mid-eighteenth century they merely held two villages as vassals of the Jaipur Raja. In the chaos of the eighteenth century these petty chieftains lent their military assistance to a variety of different masters – the Jats of Bharatpur against the house of Jaipur, then the house of Jaipur against the Jats of Bharatpur, then the shaky Moghul Emperor against predatory bands of Jat militiamen, and finally the East India Company forces against the invading Maratha armies. In this time, the fortunes of the family waxed and waned. In some years they were dispossessed vagrants, in others they were rewarded with gifts of territory. Yet by the end of the period they had fought their way free of their Jaipur

masters and made a remarkably lucky alliance with the overlords of the future, the British. In the settlement that followed the defeat of the Marathas, the British handed the Alwar Raja many bits of neighbouring territory which they were not anxious to handle themselves. The state of Alwar was in business.

But it was almost immediately ruined by dynastic collapse. There was no direct heir when the Raja died in 1815: he had failed to get round to adopting his nephew, Vinai Singh, as successor, and this gave a chance for the son of the late Raja's favourite concubine to seize the throne. The British were distressed to find their recent ally reduced to civil war between the disappointed nephew and the illegitimate usurper and tried to settle things by a share-out of the territory. This satisfied neither side and the two rivals bickered and fought intermittently for nine years until the usurper was taken prisoner and finally disinherited. But trouble quickly reappeared in 1857 when Raja Vinai Singh's death created another minority and the Alwar courtiers quickly divided into factions and got ready for civil war. The British stepped in and took direct control of the state, handing it over when the new Raja came of

The Vijay Mandir, built in 1927 beside the Vijay Sagar or lake of victory.

age, but were pretty soon back in command because the Raja could in no way control his warring courtiers. Finally when this Raja died in 1874, the ruling line was extinguished altogether. The British had to persuade the recalcitrant courtiers and clan elders to come together in conclave and elect a new ruler. They chose a minor, so there was another period of tutelary rule, and in 1892 there arose a minority yet again. In 1903, however, the Alwar line finally produced a ruler in Maharaja Jey Singh who emerged as a strong character and lasted on the throne for more than a handful of years. Yet just in case the British should be lulled into a false conviction that this carefully nurtured state had finally settled down, Jey Singh provoked a rebellion among his subjects, fell into an enormous row with his British overlords, and took off to spend his last sulky years in Paris.

As if to counter the evident shambles of their dynasty, the Alwar family managed to display all the appurtenances of princeliness in fine style. Their tiger-shoots were among the best organised, their pageantry among the most elaborate, and their palaces among the most delicate.

The tiger-hunts were so well organised because the Maharaja combined the joy of the chase with the field exercises of the Alwar armed forces. It was the ebullient, extravagant and rather irritable Jey Singh

The main courtyard of the mid-nineteenth-century City Palace. Two small temples on lotus-pattern bases flank the staircase leading to the Durbar Hall.

who perfected this particular combination. He trained his hunting elephants with particular care, ensuring that they spent several years in the reserve before they were promoted to the colours and brought into the front line. The Maharaja and his guests would set out with the Military Secretary and others of the state's top military brass aboard these mounts, while the foot soldiers and cavalry deployed through the forest around the Sariska hunting-lodge. The army engineers had prepared the ambush in advance and cleared a defile in the forest. The tigers were carefully driven into this trap by the relentless, orderly marching of the Alwar army in the military manoeuvre known as 'the beat'. The Maharaja was well-known as a crack shot, and with this well-drilled assistance he rarely missed his prey.

All the princes enjoyed their pageantry, but few arranged it with such effect as the Alwar Maharajas:

'When the Maharaja goes out in state he has the Mahi Maralib, or famous fish insignia, presented by the Emperor of Delhi to the first Chief of Ulwar, carried before him; also the images of "Sita Rama"; and he is accompanied by a person supporting a gilded umbrella, persons carrying *pankhas* [fans] representing the sun and moon, by mace-bearers, *morchal* or peacock-plume bearers, *chowie* or yak-tail bearers, men carrying curious spears, carriers of silver tiger-headed

Temples and pavilions beside the tank which brought a secure water supply to the city in the mid-nineteenth century.

clubs, runners carrying clubs and ordinary spearmen. His Highness when he goes to the feast of Dasara, uses a magnificent carriage two storeys high, drawn by four elephants; it will hold fifty people, and is elaborately gilded and decorated.'

The Alwar palace started out with several natural advantages. The craggy scenery provided a splendid setting, and the two miles of ramparts strung along the lofty rock provided a powerful backdrop to the town and palace nestling at the foot. Both the town and the palace owe a lot to Raja Vinai Singh who started to build in the 1840s after he had cleared away the threat of his rival claimant to the throne. He brought water to the city by excavating a lake outside the city, built a resplendent memorial to his predecessor who had really founded the dynasty, and finally erected the Vinai Vilas city-palace around an existing complex of temples and water-tanks. The palace was a delicate rendering of the style which had emerged out of the collision of Rajput warriors and Moghul overlords. The careful proportions of the main apartment buildings and of the magnificent Durbar hall owe much to the classic symmetry of the most famous Moghul tombs. The gateways, the *zenana*, and the proliferation of balconies go back to the fort-palaces of an earlier age of Rajput chivalry. The buildings that surround the main courtyard and palace tank are cluttered with so many varieties of arch, kiosk, portico and parapet that the effect is rather fussy; yet there is a lightness and consistency about the design which, with the help of the setting, enables the conception to survive.

Inside the palace the Alwar rulers collected together the accoutrements of Rajput civilisation. The armoury contained Raja Vinai Singh's colossal sword and lance, and also 'swords and knives with richly jewelled handles, and blades of finest steel, and shields of marvellous workmanship'. The Tosha Khana housed the state jewels (including a cup cut out of a single emerald) and state apparel. The stables contained

A frieze of Rajput miniatures sealed under glass runs along the wall of the antechamber which connects the Durbar Hall to the royal apartments.

Chatris *where the royal family cremated their dead stand above the steps to the Alwar tanks.*

some of the most thoroughbred horses from both England and India. In the late nineteenth century Raja Mangal Singh had three thousand horses. The royal library contained Sanskrit, Persian and Arabian manuscripts, and the Sheesh Mahal or mirror room was dotted with Rajput miniature painting sealed under glass. The Maharajas maintained an expensive state troupe of singers and dancers and employed a *chakhu* or taster to guard themselves against the Rajput art of poisoning.

But if Vinai Singh and his successors set out so effectively to be the very models of the Indian prince, the extraordinary Jey Singh added the final touches of quirky extravagance. He deserted the Vinai Vilas and built a new one, the Yeshwant Niwas, in an Italianate style. He then immediately decided that he did not like it, never lived in it, and began to build another, the Vijay Mandir, a monument of one hundred and five rooms, complete with temple and gardens, set beside the Vijay Sagar lake.

DUNGARPUR

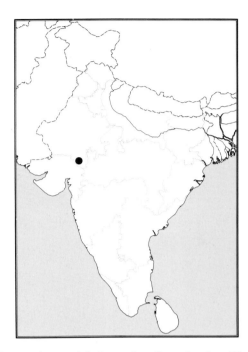

In the early thirteenth century, the Rajput chiefs and tribes had still not settled down in the hills and deserts of Rajasthan. The premier chief of Mewar (later of Udaipur) was ensconced in the great fort of Chittore, but other tribes were reluctant to honour the primacy of the fort of Mewar. Ambitious warriors fought and intrigued to take the Chittore fort, and the ruler of Mewar had to be almost constantly at war. Moreover, the Muslim invaders were already prospecting for tribute and power in Rajputana. It was a time of great disorder. The Mewar ruler lost his capital, and the family only got it back when a kinsman, who had hitherto made his name as a poet rather than a warrior, went to Sind and Afghanistan to raise an army and returned to recapture the Chittore fort. But after that short moment of glory, nine rulers were crowned in Chittore in the space of half a century – six of them died in battle, and at the end of this period Chittore was lost yet again. It was during this time of constant warfare that the state of Dungarpur became separated from the great Rajput house of Mewar.

Thus the rulers of Dungarpur claim descent from the premier Rajput clan: in the early thirteenth century, Samant Singh, the eldest son of the prince of Mewar, was cheated of his inheritance by a first cousin. Samant Singh drifted south from Chittore into the hilly area known as Bagar, which separates the mountains, valleys and deserts of Rajputana from the plains of Gujarat. It would have been foolish to migrate further, for in Gujarat there were no forts or mountain hideouts and a warrior-prince would soon be exposed to the might of Muslim soldiers. Besides, Samant Singh's mother had come from the Bagar. But it was a rough country, much less attractive than the hills and valleys of Mewar, and

94

The Udai Vilas palace seen from across the lake. On the left is an island temple which the royal family reached by boat.

The main courtyard of Udai Vilas is dominated by a four-storeyed ornamental tower. The upper room is decorated with semi-precious stones set in marble in the style of the Taj Mahal.

best known for five things – water, rocks, thorns, foul language and thieves. Much of the region was the domain of the Bhils, the fierce, wiry and primitive people who lived in the remotest hills and fought every invader down to the nineteenth century. There were also other Rajput clans who claimed possession of the hills and Samant Singh had to battle hard to gain even this unaccommodating territory. But within a century, Samant Singh's successors controlled the whole Bagar. One of them had found the great rock, seven hundred feet high, five miles in circumference and thus nearly as defensible as the rock of Chittore. His name was Dungar Singh and the capital which he founded there was called Dungarpur.

In marked contrast to the Rajput tradition of passing on family feuds from one generation to another, Mewar and Dungarpur do not seem to have remained enemies for long. As Mewar bore the brunt of the successive waves of Muslim invasion, Dungarpur chiefs lent assistance and fought alongside the princes of Mewar. Princes and warriors of Dungarpur were counted among the many thousand corpses in the fort of Chittore after the assaults of Allauddin Khalji, and among the dead left on the field of Khanva after the battle in which Babur defeated the Rajputs and laid the first foundations of the Moghul dynasty.

Like the other Rajput houses, however, Dungarpur was finally obliged to accept Moghul suzerainty. Later it suffered from the invasion of the Marathas and finally in 1818 it was gathered into a treaty with the British East India Company. By this time the state had shrunk some-

96

The four façades of the tower are identical. The doors are decorated with mirror-work. Many different elements of Rajput and Moghul architecture battle for prominence.

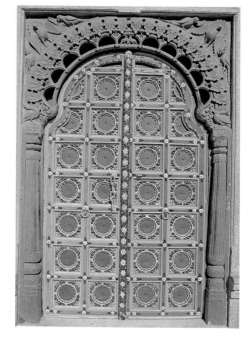

*The massive, fortified and mysterious
Juna Mahal or City Palace looms out of
the hillside.*

what. The east of the Bagar had been lost to a younger brother who formed the state of Banswara, but Dungarpur still had a mass of rough hill country and some nibbles into the margin of the plains of Gujarat.

The Juna Mahal palace built on the great rock of Dungarpur is almost as old as the town itself, and has grown steadily over the ages at the instigation of many of Dungarpur's rulers. The palace rises like a white hill above the town in a jumble of roofs, terraces, watch-towers and crenellations. It bristles with turrets, peep-holes and weapon-slits and clearly was never just a mansion: it was designed to withstand siege and to counter palace uprisings. It is honeycombed with passages which are too narrow to admit more than one man at a time, and its ceilings are kept very low so that it would be difficult to raise a sword in anger. But amongst these mementoes of warfare and family feuding, there are also touches of decoration and elegance. The principal rooms are smothered in painting and ornament; the walls and ceilings are

Craftsmen came from Udaipur to decorate the state rooms of the Juna Mahal. The floors are of chunam, *a lime plaster polished so that it resembles marble, while the walls are covered with mirror-work, fresco, Chinese tile and Rajput miniatures.*

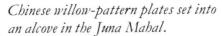
Chinese willow-pattern plates set into an alcove in the Juna Mahal.

Mirror-work in Maharaja Udai Singh's bedroom in the Juna Mahal.

painted with portraits of the ruling house and scenes from Dungarpur's history. The doors are carved with floral designs and inlaid with ebony, ivory and mirror-work; the pillars, frames and niches are carved, painted, inlaid and etched.

The explosion of colour in the interior of the Juna Mahal stands in stark contrast to the bare and battered exterior of the palace. But in fact the shabbiness of the exterior and the remarkable state of preservation of the interior both stem from the fact that since the late eighteenth century the palace has been deserted. Inside Juna Mahal there is no electricity and no modern convenience to show the effect of the past two centuries and there is almost no furniture or sign of habitation. Thus no careless shoulders have had the chance to rub away the marvellous colours of the paintings, and no clumsy servants or ebullient royal children have had a chance to damage the inlays and the carvings. In Juna Mahal the Rajput art of the sixteenth to eighteenth centuries is preserved as nowhere else.

For in the late eighteenth century the rulers of Dungarpur moved out and began work on a new palace. The turmoil of Maratha invasions and the intrusions of British empire-builders prevented these buildings reaching completion before the late nineteenth century; yet the overall conception of the original architect, Adit Ram Silawat, still dominated the construction and thus Udai Vilas shows much less influence of British colonial architecture than most of the other princely palaces built in the same period. It is set on a promontory which juts into a calm lake on the outskirts of Dungarpur town. It is approached by a long drive which winds through a jungle inhabited by herds of wild deer. The area is rich in granite and serpentine and local quarries provided the grey-green stone used in the building of Udai Vilas. The style conforms to the mixture of Rajput and Moghul which, by the eighteenth century, had become the standard fare of the princes of Rajputana; but executed in this unusual stone rather than the red or yellow sandstone it has quite a startling effect. Originally the palace buildings were arranged around a reflecting pool but this was later turned into a paved courtyard. From the middle of this courtyard there ascends an extraordinary, ornate pleasure-pavilion. The lower storey is a mass of cusped arches, busy friezes and solid-looking pillars. The second storey, which encloses a room reserved for the use of the royal women, is much more elaborate. The windows peer out from below exaggerated arcuate canopies, the balconies are supported on curvaceous brackets, the pillars are ridged, twisted and turned, and the capitals sport unusual carved figurines. Within, the walls are cool marble inlaid with semi-precious stones in the manner of the Taj Mahal. Above this there is a terrace and an encrustation of balustrades, kiosks and drooping canopies. The whole is one of the most marvellous deliberate extravaganzas in the whole of Rajput architecture.

A Rajasthani dancing girl on the walls of a state bedroom in the Juna Mahal.

Carved stone arch brought from a nearby temple to stand in the garden of Udai Vilas.

The palace has a modern wing built in 1943 but it does not intrude on the overall design. Beside this wing is a formal garden containing a marble idol and a stone arch which date back to the early years of the city. The arch was supposedly part of an enormous weighing device which was used to balance the reigning Maharaja against his own weight in gold. This weighing ceremony took place on important days in the Maharaja's life or reign, and the resulting weight of gold was distributed for charitable purposes.

Dungarpur is quite a surprise. It sits at the very edge of Rajasthan, it stayed on the outskirts of Rajput history, and it is now a bit off the beaten track of the modern traveller. Yet it contains one of the most carefully preserved of the older generation of Rajput palaces, and one of the most extravagantly unusual of the newer creations.

REWA

The rugged and jungly hills of central India first harboured the guerrilla forces of the emergent princely rulers, then became the rulers' hunting grounds, and finally were transformed into wild-life parks. Indeed, the string of game parks and bird sanctuaries that stretch through Rajasthan and central India are some of the most telling monuments to the ethos of princely rule and also a most benign gift to the Government of India tourist department. The Sawai Madhopur reserve even takes its name from a ruler of Jaipur. The Keoladeo Ghana bird sanctuary stretches away from the Bharatpur fort and used to form part of the prince's shooting domain. The Sariska game reserve was once the hunting ground of the Alwar rulers. The Udaipur rulers shot game where the Jaisamand sanctuary now lies. Rewa, meanwhile, has always been synonymous with tigers.

Originally the rough slopes of the Vindhya hills provided necessary cover for men rather than animals. In the thirteenth century an adventurer from a powerful Rajput clan in Gujarat fought his way into these hills, married a daughter of a local chief, and took up residence along with his followers in two strong forts. It turned out to be a very opportune migration, since at the end of the century the Muslim forces of Allauddin Khalji sacked their homeland of Gujarat and scattered the remaining members of the clan. Some found their way up to the two fortresses which their cousins now held deep in the Vindhya mountains. These immigrant Rajputs were known as Baghelas and the area became known as Baghelkand.

The region was so impenetrable that the Baghelas escaped the early interference of the Muslim conquerors. This happy state of affairs might

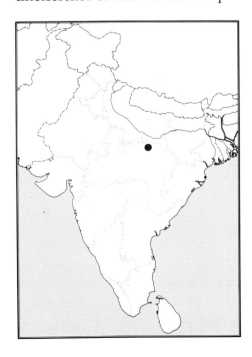

One of the five white tigers kept in the grounds of Govindgarh.

*Govindgarh, built in the late nineteenth
century on a lake surrounded by mango
groves and jungle. On the left is the
zenana, in the centre the landing stage
and terrace leading to the state rooms,
and on the right an ancient temple.*

have continued indefinitely had it not been for the fame of a singer called Tansen at the court of the Rewa ruler in his fortress of Band-hogarh. The Moghul Emperor Akbar was a lover of fine music and in 1555 he ordered Rewa to despatch the famed singer to the Moghul court. The Rewa ruler hesitated for a while, but then decided it was prudent to barter away his aesthetic pleasure in return for a little more peace. Tansen's début at Delhi was an astounding success; Akbar was 'over-whelmed' and smothered the singer with gifts. Akbar's most cultivated courtier, Abul Fazal, recorded that 'a singer the like of him has not been born for a thousand years'. When Tansen died some years later, Akbar lamented that 'music itself has expired'.

Tansen's musical talents had ended Baghelkand's isolation and before long Akbar marched in, destroyed the fortress of Bandhogarh, and brought the region under the Moghul sway. However, Moghul control was not too oppressive. Baghelkand was divided up among several subordinate chiefs, among whom the chiefs of Rewa held the first rank. The Baghela chiefs served in the Moghul armies and were rewarded with prominent positions at the Moghul court. Baghelkand was still remote, and by and large the Emperors left it alone. Under this régime, the rulers of Rewa built a new palace to replace the devastated fortress of Bandhogarh.

The Rewa palace was another Rajput city-palace built under the security of Moghul rule, and thus it contains the same merging of Rajput and Moghul styles that marks the earlier palaces of Rajasthan. The main Durbar hall, as one nineteenth-century traveller described, was 'a vast apartment, the walls of which were hidden by a profusion of gilding, incrustations in coloured glass, and ornaments of every description'. The reception halls were distinguished by the fluted columns, foliated plinths and capitals, cusped arches and arcuate lamp-niches which were the stock-in-trade of late-Moghul design, and the

Cranes and lotuses on a frieze in a bedroom of the zenana.

Durbar hall was designed to create an atmosphere of imperial power:

'Glass lustres hung from the ceiling, which was painted to represent tapestry, the teak-wood columns of the *verandah* were chequered with bright colours, and at the end of the hall was raised the throne, which consisted of an enormous velvet cushion, placed against a monumental back, and supported by two golden lions.'

Even so, this Moghul whimsy is buried deep in a palace which has all the dark, introverted character of a fortress, and whatever conception of architectural symmetry prescribed the original design, it was soon overwhelmed by a chaos of additions. The palace grew as if it had a life of its own. It acquired temples, courtyards, bathing places and a bewildering maze of halls, passageways and dungeons. There are a vast number of rooms and for most it is difficult to conceive that they ever had any real purpose. Over the whole thing later generations of Rewa rulers have dusted a layer of Victorian decorations. The result is a splendid muddle. The Rewa city-palace seems to mediate between civilisation and the disorderliness of nature; it begins life at one end in the midst of the bustling city, and runs off at the other into the maze of open jungle.

If the Baghela chiefs sent a singer as their calling-card to the Moghul rulers, they sent rather different ambassadors to the British invaders. Right up to the early nineteenth century, the jungles of Rewa harboured professional bandits – the Pindaris and Thugs. The Pindaris were freebooting soldiers who occasionally served in the armies of the Marathas but who mostly lived off plunder. The Thugs, who added a word to the English language, made a habit of murdering and robbing travellers, and then persuaded themselves that this was not just a habit but a religious duty. For four months of the year they cultivated their fields like ordinary farmers, and then for the rest of the year they practised Thuggee. Before returning to their villages for the next season's sowing, they never failed to make a pilgrimage to the temple of Bhowani at Binduchal, and there donated a fixed proportion of their 'earnings' to the goddess. The temple priests accepted the offerings without demur and blessed the givers in return. In 1812, the British discovered that the Pindaris from Baghelkand were raiding into the East India Company's territory. Moreover, the ritual component of Thuggee horrified the British just as much as the rite of *suttee*. The British imposed treaties on the rulers of Baghelkand and acquired the right to march troops through the region and to chase after the bands of Thugs and Pindaris.

Once these unpleasant characters had been dealt with, the British settled down to enjoy the other inhabitants of the Baghelkand forests. Indeed, the Rewa reserves became one of the most famous shooting spots in British India. The speciality was the tiger, and the Maharaja of

Elaborate brackets support a carved parapet at Govindgarh.

Rewa insisted that only he or his most honoured guests should have the privilege of killing them. As a result, noted one British official, 'it became almost a duty of successive Viceroys to kill a tiger or two in those famous reserves'. Less august visitors might beg for the privilege and even be allowed to go out into the jungle with a gun, but the tigers themselves would be quietly ushered away. The Maharaja, who finally handed over these preserves in 1948, had himself accounted for over eight hundred of the beasts.

Certain of the tigers were even more rigorously protected. It is difficult to imagine why anyone should think that a pale ash-blond tiger is more handsome than the usual golden variety, yet the 'white' tigers of Rewa have acquired special fame. The Maharaja let no other mortal but himself take a shot at one of these. He was also a fervent and impassioned royalist, and it was natural that he should have one of his white tigers stuffed, cased and sent as a gift to the King Emperor. He was appalled when he was later informed that this special beast had finished up, not in the corridors of Buckingham Palace, but on the shelves of the Natural History Museum in Kensington. It was not so much the royal nonchalance that offended him but the fact that such a special animal should be exposed to the vulgar gaze. A second tiger was reduced to a rug and despatched to the Palace, and distinguished visitors who happened to pass through Rewa were grilled as to whether they had seen the gift in its proper place.

In the late nineteenth century, Raghuraj Singh of Rewa built a new palace called Govindgarh in the forest about fifteen miles from the city. Appropriately enough it is a cross between a fort and a hunting-lodge. Indeed if the crenellations were Norman rather than Rajput and the decorations Tudor rather than Moghul it would be remarkably similar to the country haunts of the nobility in the highlands of Scotland. It is set in five hundred acres of forest which acted as the Maharaja's shooting reserve, and five white tigers are still kept in the courtyards.

The Old City Palace, which was originally a fort, has been added to many times since its foundation in the sixteenth century.

RIGHT *The entrance to the City Palace with the gate-house above and an array of lamp-niches on either side.*

Doric, Tuscan and Corinthian features on the façade of Jai Vilas built in the 1870s.

The Belsa gun, cast in 1602.

GWALIOR

The Rajput states had histories which stretched back long before the arrival of the British, but many of the other princely families were of much more recent origin. Indeed several were strangers to the regions which came to form their own principalities, and only rose to noble rank during the wars marking the Moghul decline and British ascent in the eighteenth century. Hyderabad, Kolhapur, Kashmir, Benares and the Sikh states of Patiala, Kapurthala and Faridkot fall into this category, as do the three great military families of the Maratha upsurge – the Gaekwads of Baroda, Holkars of Indore, and Scindias of Gwalior.

The family name of Scindia was joined to the fortified town of Gwalior in the late eighteenth century. The town's history stretches back another millennium and provides a microcosm of the turbulent history of central India, while the emergence of the Scindias illustrates the explosive rise of the hitherto peaceable Maratha peasantry of western India.

The fortress of Gwalior sits on a huge, sheer rock at the edge of Hindustan and commands the passage from the heartland of north India towards the south. It was originally built by a Rajput chieftain in the eighth century, captured by the invader Mahmud Ghazni in the twelfth, lost back to another Rajput tribe, retaken by the next Muslim raiders in the thirteenth, seized by a petty Hindu chieftain, retaken by the third wave of Muslim invaders in the early sixteenth century and finally occupied by the Moghuls in 1526. It was then tossed around between rival Moghul Emperors, princes and generals, picked up by a Jat chieftain as the Moghul Empire crumbled, and finally occupied by the Scindia family in the 1770s. But the fort's see-sawing history was not yet over. Twice the British captured it during their wars with the Marathas, and twice they handed it back. Later, after British power was finally established in India, the Gwalior troops rebelled in 1845; they joined the Great Mutiny twelve years later, and the fort was again invested by British troops. The Scindias did not get it back until 1885.

The Scindia family originated from a small village five hundred miles away to the south in Maharashtra, the land of the Marathas. Until the mid-seventeenth century, the Marathas had little or no history of military strength, but then Shivaji raised a revolt against Muslim overlordship and carved out a warrior state with the help of a guerrilla army raised from the hill peoples and peasants of western India. After Shivaji's death, the power in this state passed to the Peshwas or hereditary prime ministers. Ranoji Scindia, the son of a village headman, acquired the post of slipper-bearer at the Peshwa's court, and went on to become a high-ranking official in the state. He was succeeded by Mahadji Scindia, who became the Peshwa's greatest general, and helped push Maratha power out from the hills of Maharashtra and up through central India to the outskirts of Delhi. Just when the Marathas seemed on the point of succeeding the Moghuls on the throne of Delhi, they were halted by the invading Afghan adventurer, Ahmad Shah Abdali, and

LEFT *The pair of chandeliers in the Durbar Hall are said to be the largest in the world. Each is forty-two feet high and weighs three tons. Before they were hung, three elephants were hoisted onto the roof to make certain it would stand the strain.*

The walls and doors of the Durbar Hall are decorated with gold leaf and the heavy brocade curtains are embellished with gold thread.

A Scindia ancestor on a glass-panelled door in the private apartments.

then embroiled in the confused politicking and warring by which the East India Company soldiers gradually exerted their control over the remnants of the Moghul Empire.

Through to the end of the eighteenth century the Marathas were still a formidable force, and Mahadji Scindia's army was especially respected. This fighting force had been drilled with the help of the Comte de Boigne, a remarkable campaigner who had started out in the service of Louis XVI of France, moved from there to the army of Catherine of Russia, then to the East India Company troops, and finally to the ranks of the Company's enemy, Scindia of Gwalior. The army he made so powerful contained not only Marathas but also Afghans, Rajputs and mercenaries of every description. But in the 1790s the Maratha power was fatally weakened by a series of deaths: Mahadji Scindia succumbed to fever in 1794, the great Holkar princess Ahilya Bai died in 1795, and Nana Fadnis, who had been holding the Peshwa court together, fell to his death in the same year. The Comte de Boigne retired to his homeland the next year, and the unimpressive heirs of the Scindia and Holkar generals fought desultorily until they were finally defeated and settled by East India Company troops between 1803 and 1818.

The Scindias were allowed to retain a princedom and, after some argument, the town of Gwalior, which was by then closely associated with their name. The state of Gwalior is shaped like an arrow aimed up across central India towards Delhi and stopping just short of its target.

Maharaja Jayaji Rao built his city-palace between 1872 and 1874 when the British were still occupying the Gwalior fort after the disorders of the Mutiny. Jayaji had lived a relatively simple life which betrayed few signs of wealth and ostentation – he had even borrowed small sums of money off the British on the grounds of administrative necessity – yet after his death officials stumbled on a series of ingeniously disguised hiding places containing wealth and treasure valued at sixty-two million rupees. It was quite simply the biggest hoard of precious stones in the world, including 'silver coin that could be counted by millions, magnificent pearls and diamonds by the tens of thousands, rubies, emeralds, and other gems by thousands, and wrought and melted gold by *maunds* [an Indian measure of weight]'. This hoard of wealth possibly explains how he was able to build such a lavish palace in such haste; for Jai Vilas had to be completed at great speed in order to be ready for a visit by the Prince of Wales.

The architect was Lieutenant-Colonel Sir Michael Filose, an Indian Army man from an Indian Army family. His association with Gwalior began when he was attached to Scindia's troops during the Mutiny, but he went on to become a jack-of-all-trades in the state. He had already served as the state's head of education; later he would go on to be its first land surveyor and finally chief secretary of the Maharaja's Durbar; but in the 1870s he was trying his hand at architecture – some law-

Window in the style of art nouveau.

courts, a jail, a residence for the Scindia ladies, and the Jai Vilas palace.

Since the important purpose of the palace was the forthcoming royal visit, the showpiece of the building was naturally the Durbar hall. On the exterior the expanse of white marble was dazzling and the colossal size unavoidably impressive. But the design, which jumbled together various bits of Italian provincial architecture with exaggerated Palladian windows and an icing of Gujarati domes, was no preparation for the splendour of the interior. The enormous Durbar hall boasted two vast chandeliers with two hundred and forty-eight candles apiece. To hold these up the tall roof had to be supported on solid stone beams, and to ensure that it would withstand the strain three elephants were hoisted up to stand on the roof for several days before the chandeliers were hung in place. The remaining decoration is Italianate with a lot of gold paint, frescoes and rich brocade. As one member of a Viceregal touring party commented: 'It is like a pantomime palace with its vast chandeliers, its glass fountains, glass banisters, glass furniture and lustre fringes. But it is also very comfortable.' Another visitor added 'looks exactly like the Place Vendôme and is almost the same size'.

Like so many of the princely houses, Gwalior produced a larger-than-life character in the early twentieth century. Madhav Rao Scindia succeeded Jayaji in 1886 and endeared himself to the British by 'modernising' his state with great enthusiasm. He also recaptured some of the Scindias' flair for soldiery, maintained an elephant battery up to the First World War, and wormed his way into the British expeditionary force sent to Peking in 1900 at the time of the Boxer Uprising. He also hunted with the right amount of gusto, and was a conspicuous figure on the racecourses which became such an important part of British-Indian social life in this period. Most of all, however, he retained the playfulness of an overgrown child. This was not a new trait in the Scindia family: a British officer pressed into the disorderly celebrations of the festival of *holi* at Scindia's camp during a lull in the Maratha wars in 1804 found the Maratha general splashing his companions with water and coloured powder in the time-honoured way. 'Scindia is furnished with an engine of great power by which he can play upon a fellow fifty yards distance', wrote Sir John Malcolm. 'He has, besides, a magazine of syringes, so I expect to be well squirted.' Visitors to Madhav Rao's palace had to bear with an endless stream of pranks and practical jokes, and possibly endure a ride on the Maharaja's railway. Madhav Rao himself did the driving, as E. M. Forster rather uncomfortably noted, 'in a dashing fashion'. Other guests were taken to see the Maharaja's second railway: in the palace's enormous dining room, which was decorated with an electrically illuminated rock-garden, silver fountains playing on side-tables, and a table lit with revolving coloured balls, the guests were relieved of the effort of circulating the port and cigars by a miniature silver train that wended its way through the cutlery.

PANNA

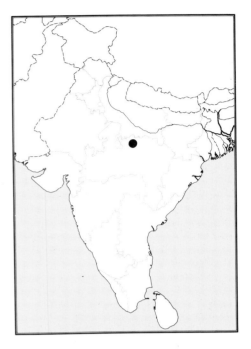

In early 1866, the French traveller Jean Rousselet was moving slowly through the hills of central India. He had already made a circuit of the great Rajput and Maratha principalities and knew well the 'form' of a visit to princely India – a reception at the hands of an overdressed prince in an over-ornate Durbar hall; some desultory conversation about the political state of Europe; a tiger-hunt for the visitor's diversion; a banquet and some party games; and then a formal and elaborate farewell. He was in a hurry to get past the hill states and on to the more promising areas such as Bhopal. The ridges of the upper Vindhyas were not only so thickly covered with jungle that passage was difficult, but they were also infamous for banditry. The Bundela inhabitants, who gave the region its name of Bundelkand, were originally Rajputs exiled from the Rajput states to the west in the fourteenth century. They had established a kingdom in the hilly area by stealth and selective murder, and gained an income by raiding down into the rich Ganges valley below the mountains. Bundelkand had harboured bandits who harassed the Moghul cities: Thugs who specialised in ritual garrotting, *dacoits* or organised highwaymen, and finally rebels from the Mutiny (Nana Sahib took refuge here after the massacre at Cawnpore). Rousselet commented: 'It is one of the least known parts of India; the evil reputation of the inhabitants, and the generally accepted opinion that it contains no monument of interest, having hitherto kept travellers away.' Rousselet's elephants almost got stuck at the river below the final ascent to the elevated plain where the state's capital stood. The Bundela state of Panna did not promise to be very hospitable.

Rousselet was in for a series of surprises. The welcome from the Panna prince, Nripat Singh, was not an august affair but a casual handshake. The prince's attire was not the usual mass of silks, brocades, military regalia and jewels, but the comparatively simple costume which was usually sported by the effete intellectuals of Calcutta rather than the heirs to a robber baronetcy. And the palace bore absolutely no resemblance to the massive baroque castles which Rousselet had just seen in the other Bundela states of Orchha and Datia. The French traveller recorded in amazement:

'It is a dwelling-place in the English style, containing several flat-roofed bungalows, surrounded with stuccoed colonnades, and broad terraces connecting together the different pavilions. The interior itself has nothing of the Indian type: and the saloon where the king received us was fitted as a study, with *escritoire*, book-case, and easy chairs.'

More was yet to come. Rousselet's party turned up at the palace on the following day in full expectation that they would be whisked off on the inevitable tiger-hunt. Instead, they were taken on a tour of the prince's kitchen garden where, talking in flawless English, the Raja pointed out the rows of cabbages and carrots which he had planted with his own

A princess of Panna descends the staircase before the nineteenth-century classical façade of the palace.

hands. He impressed on his visitors how necessary it was to improve the diet of his subjects. In the midst of a remote jungle populated by the virtually aboriginal Gound tribesmen, Rousselet had come across a ruler who lived in a *salon* atmosphere and was fanatical about vegetables.

The Raja did promise a hunt on the third day of the visit. Yet when Rousselet's party turned up in the palace courtyard in readiness for the elephant-ride into the jungle, they saw in front of the palace doorway not elephants but a steam-engine or 'road-locomotive'.

'Strange anomaly!' wrote Rousselet. 'To set out on a tiger and panther hunt in one of the wildest regions of India, and to be dragged along by a steam engine. Imagine the stupefaction of those wild Gounds – men scarcely advanced a step beyond the Stone Age – on seeing this fiery chariot, with its plumes of smoke and its storm of sparks, advancing towards their forest!'

The locomotive careered off down a specially made track while the Raja explained that it had already exploded twice and that on one of these occasions the princely house of Panna had only been saved for posterity because the Raja himself had already fallen out. The motto of the ruling house was: 'The lord of the thunderbolt is the protector of the people'.

Panna was the remnant of a much larger Bundela empire which had spread across the hills of central India between the fifteenth and seven-

teenth centuries. Three times it had fought off the inroads of a Moghul army until Shah Jehan decided to befriend these warlike people rather than fight them. But the Moghuls never really pacified these hills and the greatest of the Bundela warriors, Chhatrasal, saw no problem in serving with the Moghul army in the south of India and then immediately coming home, raising a revolt against Moghul overrule, and trying to link up with the great Maratha rebel Sivaji to drive the Moghuls out of central and western India.

The zenana *and private apartments surround a sacred tank covered with yellow water-lilies.*

Panna state actually came into existence when the Bundela territory was divided up at Chhatrasal's death in 1732. After this division, the Bundela leaders quarrelled, the Panna ruler fell out with his chief minister and with other members of his own family, and the Bundela people found themselves sadly weakened at just the time when armed strength was vital for survival. Rohilla Afghans, common bandits and the Maratha armies now pressed in from all sides. In the 1680s Chhatrasal had presented the Maratha court with an accomplished and stunningly beautiful dancer, Mastani. A hundred years later the descendants of the liaison between the Maratha chief minister and this dancer marched in and made themselves the effective rulers of most of Bundelkand. When the British arrived in the area at the turn of the nineteenth century, the ruler of Panna, Kishore Singh, was in exile.

The British restored Kishore Singh in 1811 and gave his successors the title of Mahendra and, after they had restrained this potentially troublesome area during the Mutiny, an addition of territory. The foundations of future prosperity, however, had been laid by the discovery of diamonds during the troubles of the eighteenth century. At this time Panna was the home of a holy man, Pran Nath, who preached the unity of all religions and who wrote a discourse comparing passages of similar meaning in the Hindu Vedas and the Muslim Koran. He also, according to the legend, announced that wherever Chhatrasal's horse stamped the ground, diamonds would be found. It was evidently a frisky animal for the environs of Panna are studded with small but significant diamond mines. The princely house became fabulously rich, and popular rumour supposes that ten camel-loads of diamonds are buried not far from the town.

The palace which Rousselet saw had grown in a rather haphazard manner since the restoration of Kishore Singh in 1811. It was later transformed by Nripat Singh's successor, Rudra Pratap Singh, at the end of the century. But it was a transformation which retained all the eccentricity which had so surprised Rousselet.

The transformation began with the construction of a temple to the god Balram quite near the palace. For some reason the English architect chose to model the design of this temple on St Paul's Cathedral. Rudra Pratap Singh was impressed by the result and invited the same architect to add a new western wing to the rambling palace.

This time the architect decided on a colonnaded Roman façade. He equipped it with fluted columns, Corinthian capitals, pedimented doorways and elaborate scrollwork over the porticoes, in a remarkable act of homage to the forum at Rome. The great staircase and the profusion of parapets reflected the architect's admiration for the classicism of the late nineteenth century *beaux arts* school at Paris, and indeed the design might have done very well in one of the famous *beaux arts* architectural competitions. But there were some concessions to the palace's incongruous situation which would have reduced the designer's chances of success in such a competition; for instance, the acanthus leaves which should have clustered round the Corinthian capitals had been replaced by lotus leaves. It was a folly that only an architect with dreams of Imperial grandeur could imagine, and only a prince with a diamond mine could build.

Behind the façade were the public rooms necessary for entertaining European guests. But behind them were still the rooms of the old palace. The rear opened out onto a courtyard containing an array of banyan trees and a sacred tank filled with yellow water-lilies. Around the tank lay the *zenana*, a summer pavilion and the servants' quarters. The contrast between the front and the rear of the palace is quite extraordinary. To the front is the ordered magnificence of classical Rome, curiously stranded in the jungly Vindhya hills; to the rear is the rambling spread of princely India arranged according to the demands of *purdah* and the hopes of religious salvation.

The marble-floored colonnade in the classical façade. Lotus leaves have replaced acanthus leaves in the Corinthian capitals.

INDORE

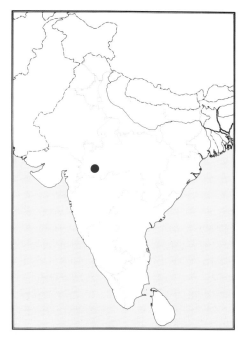

Lalbagh, the Palladian villa built outside the town on the banks of the river Szraswati in the 1920s.

Malhar Rao was born the son of a shepherd in 1693 in the village of Hol in the Maratha Deccan. By the time he died in 1766 the Holkar, or 'man of Hol', had become one of the most powerful rulers in India. He had settled his capital in the city of Indore which dominated the rich plain of Malwa, and his successors would be known as 'the Holkars of Indore'.

Malhar Rao entered the cavalry of a Maratha nobleman, impressed the Peshwa (the chief minister and effective ruling power of the Maratha state) and was elevated to the command of a cavalry regiment. Thus when the Marathas began to break out of western India and to pick up the pieces of the decaying Moghul Empire, Malhar Rao was right in the front line and well placed to take the pickings. Malhar Rao fought against several Moghul generals, against the Rajput chieftains, against the army of the Portuguese traders in Goa, and against other state-builders like the Nizam of Hyderabad. As he conquered territories, there was little to stop him taking them as his own principality. He continued to recognise the Peshwa as the overall chief of the Maratha state, and thus he formally offered his conquests to the Peshwa and then received them back as fief; but for all serious purposes they were the Holkar's dominions. Gradually he and the Scindia of Gwalior parcelled up the territories of central India, and eventually Malhar Rao Holkar was officially recognised as the Governor of Malwa. At their greatest extent, his possessions stretched from the Deccan to the Ganges.

Between this mid-century era of territorial conquest and the final collision with the British in the years from 1790 to 1818, there was a deceptive lull in the fighting. The power of the Moghuls was decisively broken, and the energies of the last Moghul armies were taken up in scrappy quarrels between tinpot rivals for the hollow Moghul crown. The British had established themselves in Bengal and Madras and were now playing elaborate diplomatic games with the French. In this period the Holkar family found another remarkable figure to consolidate Malhar Rao's gains. This was not Malhar Rao's son, who had died shortly after his father, but his daughter-in-law, Ahilya Bai.

The Maratha warrior families were noted for their strong and forceful women. Their role in history is very different from that of the Rajput noble ladies who, it seems, only emerge from the obscurity of a historical *purdah* to step onto a fatal fire either in the lonely act of *suttee* or in the grim comradeship of the *johar*. The Maratha women were more forceful, and none more so than Ahilya Bai. She was described most fulsomely by none other than Sir John Malcolm, who led many of the British diplomatic and military adventures into central India during her reign at Indore:

'It is an extraordinary picture, a female without vanity, a bigot without intolerance, a mind imbued with the deepest superstition, yet receiving no impressions except what promoted the happiness of those under her influence,

a being exercising in the most active and able manner despotic power, not merely with sincere humility, but under the severest moral restraint that a strict conscience could impose on human action, and all this combined with the greatest indulgence for the weakness and thoughts of others. In the most sober view that can be taken of her character, she certainly appears, within her limited sphere, to have been one of the purest and most exemplary rulers that ever existed.'

She built temples, fed the poor and laid the groundwork for a settled state. But when she died in 1795 central India was on the point of being overtaken by a chaos of conflicting ambitions. Indore itself added to this disorder since four brothers, grandsons of Ahilya Bai, quarrelled for the throne and their disputes left a trail of civil war, looting and wanton destruction across the wide terrain which was still counted as the Holkar's dominions. Yeshwant Rao Holkar emerged as victor, promptly marched against the Peshwa himself, and sparked off another round of warfare between the main contenders for power within the Marathas' territories while the British looked on from the sidelines.

In the time of Yeshwant Rao the fortunes of the Indore family reached their peak and then declined. He saw one of his brothers put to death by the Scindias and another by the Peshwa. He emerged from one battle against the Peshwa's troops with a spear in his side and a sabre cut across his leg. He lost an eye when a matchlock rifle exploded, and joked that it made him seem more wicked. He delighted in racing bareback on wild Maratha ponies. He knew Persian, was skilled at accounting, and was renowned as a wit. And he also had a weakness for cherry and raspberry brandy.

When the Marathas emerged from central India to prey on the remains of the Moghul Empire, one of their greatest advantages lay in their lean, mobile army. By the time the Moghul Emperors had entered their period of decline, their armies had grown too vast, pompous,

The Old City Palace in the main square of Indore.

unwieldy and slow. They were decked out with liegemen and retainers who were there for the prestige rather than for the fight, and they were weighed down with so many camp-followers that a Moghul army camp was transformed into a considerable city. The Maratha armies started out fighting fast guerrilla campaigns in the hills, and then progressed to light cavalry actions in the valleys of central India and the Deccan. They relied on speed and surprise. They exasperated the Moghuls because they refused to fight pitched battles. As the eighteenth century progressed, however, the Maratha armies also became weighed down with baggage-trains, unnecessary corps of retainers, and vast, cumbersome columns of foot-soldiers. For a short time at the turn of the century, however, Yeshwant Rao Holkar returned his army to something like the earlier mobile pattern. With this force he contained the Scindias, finally undid the Peshwa, and emerged as the most likely inheritor of the Maratha gains. But then he came up against a military force which was

even more light, mobile and perhaps better equipped – the forces of *The throne room at Lalbagh.*
the East India Company. Between 1803 and 1805 Yeshwant Rao cut a
swathe across north-western India, but the Company forces were able
to deflect him away from Delhi, and push his course up towards the
emergent Sikh warrior-states of the Punjab, where a Maratha was just
as much an unwelcome invader as were the British 'hat-men'. Hemmed
in on all sides, the Holkar finally agreed to a treaty. Yeshwant Rao still
rejected the idea of a division of territories: 'My country and property
are upon the saddle of my horse,' he told the British colonel who was
negotiating the settlement, 'and please God, to whatever side the reins of
the horses of my warriors may be turned, the whole of the country in
that direction shall come into my possession'. He was not allowed such
latitude, yet it was the peace made with the Holkar in 1806 which
effectively ensured that Rajasthan and central India would remain the
domain of the princes and would not be absorbed into British India.
The clashes with Holkar had persuaded the British to retire behind the
Yamuna river and to consolidate their possessions while allowing the
Maratha and Rajput princes to rule in the territory beyond.

An English-style fireplace in the dining room at Lalbagh.

There was still another war and another treaty in 1818 before the settlement was confirmed, and in this time the territories of Indore shrank. Yeshwant Rao Holkar's army grew steadily in size after the containment of 1805-6 and finally rebelled because it was not being paid. Yeshwant Rao turned more and more to his cherry and raspberry brandy in remorse, and finally lost his senses. His successor, another Malhar Rao, was just eleven years old when the Company army dealt the final blow to the Holkar's forces in 1818. The young boy, seated on a war elephant, burst into tears when his troops were forced into retreat.

The Holkar armies had once ranged up into the Punjab, across into the Ganges valley and down into Rajasthan where many of the Rajput princes were forced to pay tribute. The final settlement of 1818 forced the Holkar back onto the plain of Malwa, the region which the founder Malhar Rao had taken when he had first crossed the Narmada valley in the northwards surge of the Maratha troops. It was a small domain, but it was rich. It was watered by two good rivers and it grew both the cotton and, more importantly, the opium, which soon became the staples of western India's foreign trade.

Reflection of the Italianate ceiling of one of Lalbagh's many anterooms.

An immense Aubusson carpet covers the floor of the anteroom.

The Holkars were subdued but they were far from pacified, and throughout the period of British rule the state of Indore gave the British a deal of trouble. A bloody succession dispute followed Malhar Rao II's death in 1833. The Indore troops rebelled and joined the Mutiny in 1857. The British found it necessary to force the Holkar to resign his throne in favour of his son in 1904. And in 1924 the reigning Holkar came uncomfortably close to being implicated in the well-publicised murder of a playboy millionaire in Bombay; again the British forced the Holkar to abdicate in favour of his son. Finally the Holkar refused to adopt the right tone of loyalty towards the British cause during the Second World War. With great dedication, the family of Indore became the truculent mavericks of princely India.

And yet, like so many other princely families, when they came to build a new palace they chose an architectural style that paid fulsome homage to the Europe of their unwanted masters. The eighteenth-century Old Palace was a vast walled mansion distinguished by a

The only room in Lalbagh which is not European in style is the hall where the dancing girls performed. At the centre is a silk Persian carpet.

seven-storey gateway, and both mansion and gateway were built in the style of the town-house of western India, only on a vastly inflated scale. At the end of the nineteenth century, Shivaji Rao Holkar filled Indore with a new array of palaces. The New Palace, which stood beside the Old in the centre of the city, was the inspiration of the Maharani, whom a British official described as 'very much the type of the modern English public-school girl, a good tennis player and very up-to-date in fashions of dress'. The gateway bore an unlikely resemblance to the entrance to Buckingham Palace, while the interior was like 'a modern English country house equipped with all the latest conveniences – electric kitchens, electric heating, a cocktail bar and so forth'. The Lal Bagh palace was built to the south on the banks of the Saraswathi river, and the Manik Bagh palace was located even further out. Lal Bagh was designed by Mr Triggs of Calcutta who, it was said, was 'determined to incorporate all the architectural ideas of Europe in an Indian setting'. He appears to have come perilously close to success.

KOLHAPUR

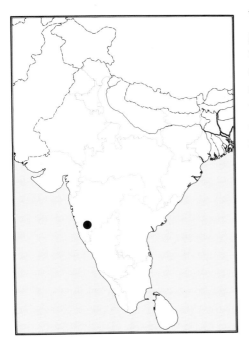

A hybrid clocktower dominates the frontage of Charles Mant's palace at Kolhapur.

While the states of Gwalior, Indore and Baroda are the residue of the great Maratha military expansion of the eighteenth century, Kolhapur is the last trace of the founding father of Maratha power, the seventeenth-century warrior, Shivaji. He died in 1680 after pushing the Moghuls out of western India and beginning the process of Moghul decline. But when he died the Moghuls were still strong enough to take their revenge on his successors. The Moghul armies hemmed the Maratha forces into the mountainous fringe of the western Deccan and stood by while Shivaji's powerful state was riven by internal disputes. Shivaji had left no clear successor and for thirty years after his death two separate lines of descent, goaded by ambitious queens and courtiers, fought for precedence. Eventually, in 1710, the two parties managed to establish a shaky territorial boundary between their possessions. The line descending from Shivaji's elder son settled its capital at Satara, took the northern Maratha country, and acquired the right to expand to the north. Yet in Satara the princely family was soon forced into the backseat: the hereditary minister, the Peshwa, took over the reins of power, and his generals forged out to the north and formed the Maratha princedoms. Meanwhile, the line descending from Shivaji's younger son took the southern territories and the right to expand to the south. They settled in the great fort of Panhala, amid the craggy peaks and deep valleys of the hills of the Western Ghats, and later transferred their capital to the ancient city and trading capital of Kolhapur.

The southern frontier turned out to be less profitable than the northern one. While the Satara armies, which started raiding north from the Maratha country in the early eighteenth century, found that the remnants of Moghul grandees and Rajput princes were easy pickings, the Kolhapur armies faced other powerful emergent princes in the south – the Nizam of Hyderabad, the Mysore armies of Hyder Ali and Tipu Sultan, and the Moghul warmonger, Zulfikar Khan. The Kolhapur forces were more or less confined to their mountain retreat, occasionally harassed by Moghul armies, and reduced to snapping at the heels of their more expansive cousins from Satara.

Against this rather unhappy background the princely line of Kolhapur turned into a dynastic disaster. Time and time again the Kolhapur prince failed to produce an heir, or died when the heir was only a few years old. Sometimes it was the toll of war which brought about this unfortunate state of affairs, but sometimes it was a streak of insanity which dogged the family; and sometimes just an inability to survive to any great age in the dark fortresses amid the sticky sub-tropical forests of the Western Ghats. Each time the failure to provide a clean succession created an opportunity for rivalries, ambitions and debilitating succession disputes.

In the early nineteenth century, Kolhapur was just as uneasy under British control as were the other Maratha states of Gwalior and Indore.

The tiger heads and silverware in the trophy room reflect the present Maharaja's passion for hunting big game and breeding racehorses. In 1965 his horses scooped the three Indian classics.

At first the British tried to settle the state by force. Company troops invaded in the 1820s, again in the 1840s when the outlying areas of the state rose in revolt; and in 1857 the Kolhapur troops mutinied. After the Mutiny, however, the British guardians changed their tactics and decided to use the book rather than the gun to bring Kolhapur to heel. This strategy had its own difficulties because of the mortality rate of the Kolhapur heirs. The British invested great care and attention in the education of two Kolhapur heirs who, before they could ascend the throne and emerge from their British-made chrysalis as 'model rulers', were gathered to their forefathers. It was not until Shahu Chhatrapati ascended the throne in 1894 that the policy finally paid off. Under Shahu and later under his son Rajaram, Kolhapur acquired the social reforms and public buildings which the British so liked to see in the 'Native' states. Moreover, Kolhapur became renowned as a centre of outdoor sports, notably the exotic business of pig-sticking; and an extraordinary

A silver chair belonging to the Kolhapur royal house.

form of hunting deer: Rajaram imported cheetahs from Africa and used these animals to hunt the herds of black buck in the hills and valleys of the Western Ghats. The Maharaja drove an enormous horse-drawn wagon across the rough terrain in pursuit of the black buck and, when he had succeeded in separating his prey from the herd, his attendants removed the hoods from the cheetahs and allowed them to bound out of the wagon, overhaul the unlucky buck, and bring it to the ground.

The British guardians, who appreciated the sportiveness and progressiveness of reformed Kolhapur, also urged the building of a new palace. The capital had shifted from the fort of Panhala to the town of Kolhapur in 1788, and in 1810 the old fortified palace at Kolhapur was badly damaged by fire: at the time when the British forces were all set to overwhelm Kolhapur, some of the prince's Pathan mercenaries complained about the failure of the state to pay their salaries, imprisoned the prince's ministers, and when loyal troops besieged the rebels in the palace, the Pathans set fire to the carpets and burnt a large part of the building to the ground. The palace was later repaired, but in the latter part of the century the British guardians felt that the Kolhapur ruler should have a new residence to suit the education and refinement which they were so zealously forcing upon him. The architect they chose was Major Charles Mant of the Royal Engineers.

Mant had first come out to India in 1859 and had quickly emerged as one of the most remarkable young architects working in India. His first designs strongly derived from European models and the high school he built at Surat was a careful imitation of Italian Gothic architecture. Soon after he began his association with Kolhapur and built a town hall also in an Italian Gothic style. But before he had been in

India for very long he became fascinated by local architecture and set out, according to one of his foremost official patrons, 'to unite the usefulness of the scientific European designs together with the beauty, taste, grandeur and sublimity of the native style'. In the following years, he became one of the greatest exponents of the 'Indo-Saracenic' style – a term which was applied to a synthesis of Muslim and Indian features, generally perpetuated by European architects. In this style he designed a large number of schools, halls and other public buildings for several of the princely rulers, including a hospital and high school at Kolhapur. He also built an Indo-Saracenic monument in Florence where the young Kolhapur heir had died in 1870 while still in the course of his European education. His first design for a palace came at Cooch Behar in 1875, but the structure was not built on grounds of too high a cost. He later went on to produce designs for the Maharajas of Darbhanga, Baroda and Kolhapur, but did not live to see any of these designs completed. While all three palaces had simultaneously reached little farther than the foundations, he lost control of his senses, became convinced that his palatial designs would fall down because he had done the sums wrong, and died tragically while still in his forties.

The palaces of course stood up perfectly well. The Kolhapur palace was built out of grey stone and arranged around a central courtyard. Mant drew the plans for the layout and elevation, but left it to the native draughtsmen to design the details of ornamentation. By the time he came to this commission, Mant had progressed beyond the rather formal intricacies of the Indo-Saracenic style, and was intent on incorporating as much as possible of the local architecture of the region in which the buildings were to be placed. So at Kolhapur he copied elements from several sources. In the town of Kolhapur itself there were some famous ancient temples to the goddess Mahalakshmi and an impressive Nagarkhana or drum gate on the old palace. Next there were the Jain temples, particularly those at nearby Ahmedebad. The Jain religion, an offshoot from the same original stock as Hinduism and Buddhism, had always been particularly strong in western India and had counted many of the Maratha ruling families amongst its adherents. The skyline of the Kolhapur palace was distinguished by the multiple, clustered domes copied from the design of the Ahmedebad temple towers, and by the tall clocktower which recapitulates the idea, and some of the detail, of the towers of victory which the Jains built in many of the old forts (two of which still survive in the fort of Chittore). Finally there were the old hill fortresses at Bharatpur, Deeg and Mathura. Mant chose these particular sources because they were all examples of local architecture which had preceded, or been relatively little influenced by, the artistic innovations of the Muslim invaders. Mant wanted to make his Maratha buildings a tribute to the Maratha resistance to Moghul rule.

The influence of Jain architectural styles is evident in this tower seen from the porticoed entrance to the palace.

The crescent of Islam stands out
incongruously on the severely Italianate
façade of Falaknuma.

Built by a local nobleman, purchased by
the Nizam to please a favourite queen,
it was left empty during most of its
hundred years of existence.

HYDERABAD

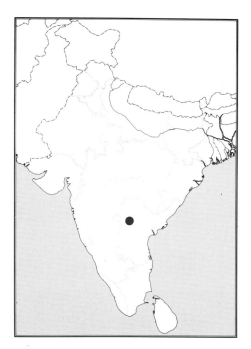

The genealogy of the Asaf Jah dynasty of Hyderabad is one of the most illustrious and ancient in the Muslim world. In the eighteenth century they joined together a line of descent on the male side from the first Khalipha, the Prophet Mohammed's successor, and on the female side from the Prophet himself. Their domain, however, was the rocky expanse of the southern Deccan, and four-fifths of their subjects were Hindus. Like the Maratha princedoms, the state of Hyderabad was created amidst the decay of the Moghul Empire, but unlike the Maratha rulers the Nizam of Hyderabad was a Muslim, a member of an immigrant family, and a servant and appointee of the Moghul Emperor. Indeed after 1857, the Nizam became the last surviving memento of Moghul rule. Therein lay problems for the future.

If the first Nizam could claim such an illustrious descent back to the time of Islam's foundation, he could also claim a more recent and still prestigious descent from one of the premier families of central Asia. His grandfather had been the leading noble in the city of Samarkand. His father, Khwaja Abid, visited India on his pilgrimage to Mecca in 1654, fell in with the forces of Aurangzeb, and before long had emerged as one of Aurangzeb's most trusted generals. Khwaja Abid passed this honour on to his son, Mir Kamruddin Khan, who helped Aurangzeb to fulfil the long-held ambition of the Moghuls to extend their conquest to the south of India. In 1713 Mir Kamruddin Khan was appointed governor of the Moghul province of the south, and given the title of Nizam-ul-mulk or Regulator of the State. Ironically, this very conquest had finally stretched the boundaries of the Moghul Empire beyond manageable limits. The Empire began to crumble and soon the Moghul appointee in the Deccan had become an independent ruler. Mir Kamruddin Khan settled his capital at Hyderabad, retained his Moghul title, and began the Asaf Jah dynasty as the Nizam of Hyderabad.

At this stage his rule extended over almost all of peninsular India. But the second half of the eighteenth century was not so glorious. Like many new dynasties, the Asaf Jahs immediately faced terrible problems over succession. Mir Kamruddin Khan died in 1748; his successor was assassinated in 1750; the third Nizam was murdered a year later; the fourth was poisoned by the mother of the fifth, who survived only two years before he in turn was dethroned and killed by his younger brother. While the family tree was being hacked about in this manner, the Deccan was becoming a cockpit for ambitious imperialists. Hyderabad lost territory to the French, British, the Marathas and to Mysore, before limping into a treaty with the East India Company in 1779. But this still left the Nizam with the biggest of all the native states besides the mountainous expanse of Kashmir. By the twentieth century, the state of Hyderabad had twenty million people. The British recognised it as the premier native state, and called its ruler His Exalted Highness and their 'faithful Ally' – for Hyderabad had narrowly remained loyal in the Mutiny and this was largely due to the actions of the reigning Nizam.

However, after the British had replaced the Muslim Moghuls as the dominant power in the subcontinent, the position of the immigrant Muslim ruler in the midst of his overwhelmingly Hindu population became increasingly awkward. Through the nineteenth century a series of capable administrators, notably Salar Jung, hauled the state back from bankruptcy and introduced the necessary accoutrements of material and social progress. But the Nizams locked themselves in their palace of King Kothi in the centre of Hyderabad and surrounded themselves with Muslim courtiers and servants. The palace was large. It was divided off from the outside world by rings of dull, brown walls, and the visitor entered through a series of vast courtyards before he reached the Nizam's apartments. The sprawl of outbuildings – the palace covered nearly half a square mile – housed almost ten thousand

The façade of Falaknuma.

persons in various degrees of discomfort. There were relatives, wives, concubines and their offspring, courtiers, functionaries, some two thousand servants, and a platoon of Amazons dressed in brown uniforms of French design standing guard over the *zenana*.

After the collapse of the old Muslim capital at Delhi and the overthrow of other Muslim princes and viceroys throughout India, Hyderabad emerged as the last remnant of the Moghul era. Many Muslim nobles and merchants drifted south to settle in Hyderabad and to build their own palaces and town houses in and around the complex of King Kothi. Moreover Hyderabad still acted as part of 'the Muslim world' rather than of the Indian subcontinent and continued to attract immigrants from Arabia, Abyssinia, Turkey, Persia and central Asia just as Muslim north India had done over the past five centuries. Some of the immigrants were nobles, some merchants, and some poets and craftsmen to adorn the Nizam's court. Meanwhile, Arab mercenaries came to serve in the Nizam's army, which acted rather like a Praetorian Guard or corps of janissaries. Hyderabad became a very introverted city, a little Muslim island in a Hindu ocean. There even arose a term, *mulki*, which described the inhabitants of Hyderabad as opposed to the dwellers in the outside world. And they still use the term 'Moghlai' to describe the administration of princely Hyderabad (as opposed to the British administration over most of India), and also to describe the variant of rich Persian-style cooking which was favoured by the prosperous inhabitants. 'There is an atmosphere of old-world culture and refinement', wrote one British official, 'such as I have come across nowhere else in the world save in Pekin. It is perhaps more Persian than Indian.'

The tenth Nizam, Mir Usman Ali, was the last to rule over this isolated and gently decaying culture. From 1911 to 1949 he came to symbolise the cloistered anachronisms of this remnant of medieval history. By nature he was a shy and taciturn man who disliked the gaudy pageantry of princely India, who avoided the Viceregal round and the desperate socialising between the British rulers and their princely charges, and who communicated with the outside world as little as possible. Yet his position and his wealth were such that whatever he did or did not do became a matter of public interest and often official concern as well. He was one of the richest men in the world, and his wealth was somehow especially exciting because it was not tucked away in bills and bonds, but piled up in stacks of gold bricks, chests of diamonds and pearls, and mountains of silver rupees. Moreover his wealth kept increasing almost as a matter of course: because of his exalted lineage and his role as the last standard-bearer of Muslim power in India he was deluged with *nazars* of offerings from the nobles clustered around his court in Hyderabad and from men of the faith throughout India and beyond. Such wealth created rumours. People talked of the three hundred expensive motor cars which had been presented by

The Nizam has a famous collection of jade. This gold-embellished box contained the ingredients for the Indian sweetmeat pan.

the Nizam's admirers and which now rusted in the stables of King Kothi. Others passed on the news that visitors had seen a famous diamond called 'Jacob' being used as a paperweight.

An even more exciting topic of gossip than the Nizam's wealth was the Nizam's parsimony. Visitors to tea were supposedly rationed to one biscuit each, while the Nizam smoked only the cheapest of cigarettes, rode in a battered Buick while the ranks of Rolls-Royces decayed in the stables, wore the same cap for thirty years and carried the same walking stick for forty. He dressed so shabbily that incautious visitors mistook him for a servant.

In fact Mir Usman Ali was a good deal more complex than the popular legend suggested. Despite his famous niggardliness, and despite the antagonism he occasionally showed towards his British masters, on the outbreak of the Second World War he immediately presented the RAF with a squadron of Hurricane fighters and the navy with a corvette. Even though he lived a spartan life at home and took his position as a leader of Islam very seriously, he was quite capable of being convivially bibulous in the company of the English Resident.

He did not even use Falaknuma, the palace which stood on the hill overlooking the city. It had been built in 1872 as the private residence of one of Hyderabad's richest Muslim grandees. Mir Usman Ali's predecessor as Nizam had purchased it to please his favourite queen, but she soon tired of it. After 1911 it became the Nizam's guest-house but it was barely used because the Nizam had hardly any guests. For odd weeks it housed a touring Viceroy and once or twice it was graced by British royalty. For the rest of the time it was immaculately maintained but stood magnificently empty. It had been a sumptuous building in the first place and Mir Usman Ali's predecessor had added a new wing to convert it from a noble to a royal residence. This entailed tacking a Saracenic jumble on to the back of the severely mock-classical

Hidden from sight at the rear of Falaknuma are the Moorish arches, parapets and domes of the zenana.

The furniture of the zenana *is made of sandalwood and inlaid with ivory. It was commissioned from the Muslim craftsmen of Kashmir.*

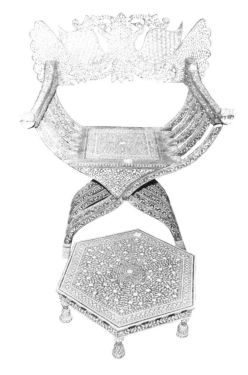

136

original building in order to accommodate the *zenana*. The result aroused predictably strong reactions. 'A pile of whitewashed stucco without style or distinction,' scoffed Prevost Battersby who, if anything, saw it at its best, decked up for the visit of a British royal prince in 1906. 'It is considered the finest in India,' blandly reports Murray's guide and goes on to describe its artistic merits: the fine gateway at the end of a winding drive through the hills, the ancient trees, the formal English garden, 'the Grecian façade with the cornice resting on the double row of Corinthian columns; the handsome vestibule . . . fitted with marble seats surrounding a marble fountain . . . the marble staircase with the beautifully carved balustrades supporting, at intervals, marble figures with candelabra'. There is also an oriental library with a ceiling of carved and painted wood and a priceless collection that includes one of the earliest copies of the Koran. The rooms were furnished in Italian

The grand marble staircase is lined with portraits of the governor-generals and viceroys of British India.

A hookah *for four smokers stands in the library. The base is of silver inlay.*

and French styles, relieved occasionally by some fine Kashmiri furniture, and everywhere were packed with Victorian bric-à-brac.

Since Mir Usman Ali hardly used the building, it remains as a monument to his predecessor, and has been painstakingly preserved as it was when he died in 1911. Until recently, his favourite dog still sat in one of the drawing rooms and stared out at the bare rooms through his glass eyes. The only changes have been grudging concessions to the comforts that were presumed to be required by Falaknuma's more illustrious guests. In 1906, Queen Mary's bathroom was fitted with a spray for perfume. In 1912, the future Duke of Windsor was allowed to enjoy the innovation of electric lights.

When the British prepared to leave India, this remnant of Moghul decline ceased to be a funny anomaly and became a political problem. The Nizams had always resented the British yoke and in 1926 Mir Usman Ali made a lame attempt to assert his own independence. Then when in the 1940s a British officer informed him that the British were on the point of departure, 'He bounced up in his seat and with a gleeful grin said, "You mean I can do then as I like?"' The princely states were invited to merge themselves into one of the emergent countries of India or Pakistan. The worst thing that anyone could predict was that the orthodox recluse who ruled Hyderabad might try to attach his state to Pakistan: the population of Hyderabad was eighty per cent Hindu and the state was completely surrounded by Indian territory, so that such a move would clearly have created problems. However, the Nizam exceeded even these gloomy expectations, and decided Hyderabad would merge in neither of the two countries but would proceed instead as an independent territory.

Mir Usman Ali perhaps knew the testament which the first Nizam had left on his death in 1748 to act as a guide to the future rulers of Hyderabad. In this testament, he surveyed the peoples of India and concluded: 'the inhabitants of Gujarat and the Frontier Province of Kashmir are considered a bad lot. It is necessary to avoid them and guard against them, and not believe what they say in season or out of season.' The two men who were luring the princes to merge their territories into India were the Prime Minister, Jawaharlal Nehru, who was a Kashmiri Brahmin, and the Home Minister, Sardar Patel, who came from Gujarat. Anyway, the Nizam rejected the blandishments of these two men, appealed to the United Nations, started minting his own coinage and policing his borders. He formed a ministry consisting of some of the most *mulki* of his courtiers and set out to defy the outside world. Eventually the Indian government gave up the use of words and sent in the troops. Hyderabad became part of India, and the Nizam was treated like all the other princes. He died in 1967, still complaining that his tax-free pension of five million rupees a year (plus the wealth from estates and treasure chambers) left him a poor man.

MYSORE

Many indulgent pilgrimages to southern India have finished up at Mysore. A refugee north Indian prince came in the fourteenth century, chivalrously killed a local warlord, married the daughter of the man whom he thus restored to his rightful petty kingdom, and so founded the Wadiyar dynasty of Mysore. The Muslims came from north India in search of loot and war-elephants but were dissuaded by the harsh terrain and the fiercely independent Hindu inhabitants. Later foreign visitors came from British India and beyond to enjoy the spectacular entertainments laid on by one of the most famous and hospitable Maharajas. Even now people come from all over India and from much farther afield to see the natural beauties – mountains, rivers and waterfalls – and man-made wonders – temples, statues and palaces – of this unusual corner of southern India.

The Wadiyar family played an important role in south Indian history from the fourteenth to eighteenth centuries. Then just when they were preparing themselves to resist the invasion of Muslim power from the north, they were turned out of their kingdom by an attack which came from an entirely unexpected direction: in 1759 a Muslim junior officer in the Wadiyars' own army, Hyder Ali, rose in revolt, imprisoned the Raja and his family and proclaimed himself king. Hyder Ali then allied with the Marathas, hired French military advisers, and set off on a career of brilliant victories which seemed sure to make him the ruler of all southern India.

But by the late eighteenth century too many forces were interested in the political future of south India and spectacular military expeditions were not enough. By the time Hyder Ali died in 1782 he had

Amba Vilas palace. On the left of the monumental gateway is one of the palace's four temples. The domes are covered with eighteen-carat gold.

The Maharaja's personal regiment of horse changes guard.

already fallen out with the Marathas and lost a crucial battle with the British. His son, Tipu Sultan, continued to harass the East India Company's forces but in 1799 he was finally forced back into his capital at Seringapatam, attacked, defeated and killed.

The British then dug out a five-year-old Wadiyar boy, a remnant of the dynasty which Hyder Ali and Tipu Sultan had displaced, placed him on the throne, sent out a distinguished military officer, Captain Wilks, to write a history of the region and to make sure the lad's genealogical antecedents were perfectly in order, and without a trace of irony appointed the Brahmin minister who had been the trusted lieutenant of both Hyder and Tipu to look after his administration. The overall supervision of this extraordinary settlement was the first governmental charge of the man who went on to become the Duke of Wellington and a prime minister of England. He had just turned thirty at the time.

But while this British overseer settled in to Tipu's old palace at Seringapatam, the new Wadiyar dynast, Krishnaraja, settled in a less turbulent spot under the shadow of another bit of sacred geography, the Chamundi Hill, and built up a capital at the town of Mysore.

The Wadiyars had been presented with the third largest of the Indian states, and decided to run it in a highly unusual way. They built a separate administrative capital at Bangalore, left most of the administration to capable professionals, and even welcomed the establishment of legislatures and other appurtenances of democratic government. Thus while the politicians and bureaucrats ensured that the people got a fair share of bread, the Maharaja himself took care of the circuses. Although many of the great occasions were reserved for the Maharaja's distinguished guests, some were also public and Mysore gained a reputation for well-managed spectacle.

The most public of these was the festival of Dasara which traditionally marked the end of the 'season of rain' and the beginning of the 'season of warfare'. For this occasion the Maharaja went out in state to the temple on Chamundi Hill and was, temporarily at least, transformed into a god. At the end of a few days, the Maharaja processed back to his capital, was discreetly and privately deprived of his divinity, and inaugurated an orgy of celebration. The Mysore palace was smothered in the light of thousands of little oil-lamps, much of the town followed suit, and seemingly most of the population of the state trekked into the capital to revel in the spectacle.

The Maharaja took even more care over his private entertainments. He kept an English Military Secretary to plan dinners, dances and tennis parties, and an English Private Secretary to organise musical evenings, equip the palace's chamber orchestra, and occasionally play second fiddle to the Maharaja's first violin. But the most famous of the Maharaja's more private entertainments was the Khedda or elephant round-up. It was elephants that had drawn the Muslims to the south, had formed the mainstay of Mysore armies, and had latterly become the symbol of the Wadiyar ruling family. Mysore elephants also gained a widespread public fame. It was Airawat, a Mysore elephant, that the world saw in the role of Kipling's Kala Nag and it was in Airawat's careful trunk that Sabu learnt to be an elephant boy. The Khedda became the high-point of the 'Mysore Week' which had the same place on the social calendar of British India as did 'Ascot Week' back home. The Kheddas were originally staged to round up herds of wild elephants which were devastating the countryside and which could usefully be put to work, but they became an entertainment for visiting dignitaries. The operation began three months before the grand finale, with teams of elephant hunters driving the wild herd slowly towards a prearranged trap. The visitors came to see the last operation when about a hundred tame and trained elephants and about five thousand men drove the wild beasts into a stockade where they were hobbled and led away for domestication and training. The sheer power of the wild elephants, the fighting spirit of their leading tuskers, the patient manoeuvring of the tame elephants, the skill of the trainers skipping around the legs of the vast beasts to apply the hobbles, and the nervous anticipation of the visitors who were separated from the beasts by nothing more than a flimsy bamboo stockade, added up to an extraordinary event. To ensure the pleasure of his guests, the Maharaja somehow managed to provide electricity, running water, an orchestra and other creature comforts in the depths of the jungle.

Naturally enough, a ruling family so dedicated to fantastic entertainments had a string of equally fantastic palaces. The first was built in the fort of Mysore but there was soon added an English-style mansion at the nearby hill resort of Ootacamund to act as a summer residence, a palace at the administrative capital of Bangalore in a design that deliber-

LEFT *The extravagant throne room, built in the early years of this century, has astonished every visitor.*

One of the glories of Mysore is its stained glass. Peacocks adorn the roof of the throne room.

Birds fly across the octagonal roof of the council chamber.

The ranks of pillars in the throne room resemble the many-pillared halls of the south Indian temples.

ately recalled Windsor Castle, and a white Italianate villa on the top of the Chamundi Hill to accommodate the family during devotional periods. But the main palace was built after the old residence in the Mysore fort had been partially destroyed by fire in 1897. It was deliberately enormous and lavish – the Durbar hall could seat a thousand people – but it was also deliberately curious, for its architectural inspiration has an extraordinary ancestry.

The south could boast few solidly built palaces before the eighteenth century, and most of the monumental architecture in the region had been confined to temples. The men who carved the stone for the new Amba Vilas palace in Mysore were the heirs to a local tradition of stone-carving made famous in temples such as those at nearby Belur and Halebid. Many features of both overall design and detail from temple architecture have thus found their way into the Mysore palace. Traditionally the temple, which was reckoned as the 'palace of god', stood at the centre of the town and acted as the focus of the system of streets. In like manner, the thoroughfares of Mysore city converge at the Amba Vilas palace's triumphal gateway. Furthermore, the southern temples had distinctive covered arenas known as 'thousand-pillar halls' and relied heavily on rows of elaborately sculpted pillars to mark the progress towards the deity. The Mysore palace is built round a spacious courtyard ringed by rows of massive stone pillars, each one carved in an elaborate design.

But after this the temple influence stops and many other influences intervene. The palace was, oddly enough, designed by an English architect called Irwin who had built many public buildings in Madras. In that city he had experimented with the blend of Muslim designs and Indian materials which, generally in the hands of British architects, became known an Indo-Saracenic. It is a curious hybrid style which could only come out of the efforts of men of one culture trying to understand and synthesise the jumbled legacy of another. Anyway, it meant that Mr Irwin hurled into the Mysore palace fluted pillars and foliate capitals from the Delhi fort, onion domes from the Taj Mahal, arcuate canopies from the Rajput palaces, and topped everything with a fantastic campanile of mixed Italian and Indian provenance. In the interior, the temple corridors vied with stately European halls, and elaborately carved ceilings jostled with the florid tracery of a Moghul interior. Pink and green paint, stained glass windows, and the furnishings of early twentieth-century Europe completed the picture. And it all seemed to work. 'In effect', wrote one dazzled European visitor, 'there seems not an inch of repose on all its surface, it is all curves and carvings.' As for the Durbar hall, 'Out of its own setting this hall would be unbearable; safely within, it has real fitness and beauty'.

Prevost Battersby saw the palace while it was under construction in 1905, and he noted how the Maharaja was ensuring that the act of

The colossal Nandi bull on the slopes of the Chamundi hill where the Maharaja worshipped every day of the year.

building was not merely a piece of self-indulgence but served as yet another entertainment for his subjects:

Sunset over the Amba Vilas palace.

'The place resounded to the mallet, the chisel was everywhere eating its way into uncompleted carvings; chips of granite flew from the low-vaulted roofs; the floors were littered with men at work upon blocks of marble, slabs of porphyry, junks of teak, and panels of sandalwood, intricate lattices and delicate inlay, on ivory doors and jambs of silver; yet there was no attempt made to exclude the public, whether it came in a loin cloth or a black silk coat. Men, women, and children, the whole populace streamed in, watching with wondering eyes the brown teak turn to birds and flowers, and the shapes of gods and beasts grow out of the green serpentine; shook the granite chips from their hair, brushed the dust and the mire of masonry from their *saris*, humbly removed themselves when found in the way, and so wandered on from room to room.'

BARODA

The state of Baroda emerged, like Indore and Gwalior, from the Maratha military explosion of the eighteenth century. Like the Holkars of Indore and the Scindias of Gwalior, the Gaekwads of Baroda trace their family back to a humble origin – though the family name, Gaekwad, meaning protector of cows, refers to an act of religious merit not a hereditary occupation as a drover – and can attribute their later glory to military prowess in the service of the Maratha Peshwa. In 1720 Damaji Gaekwad was made deputy commander of the Maratha army as it pushed north-west into the fertile lands of Gujarat. By 1731 Damaji's nephew and successor, Pilaji Gaekwad, had pushed the Moghul forces out of Gujarat and in 1734 had captured the town of Baroda. His son moved the capital there in 1766.

The Gaekwads were singularly happy with their new domain in Gujarat. It was one of the richest agricultural regions in the Indian subcontinent. Thus while the Holkars and Scindias spent the rest of the eighteenth century forging out into upper India and forever skirmishing with the British, with the Sikhs, with the Rajputs and with one another, the Gaekwads were generally content to consolidate their position in Gujarat and to extend their sway down into the peninsula of Kathiawad. Of course, the Baroda forces joined in the major Maratha campaigns, but they devoted the greater part of their energies to keeping their nominal overlord, the Peshwa, out of the rich lands of Gujarat. At the end of the century they were embroiled in the intricate diplomacy and scrappy campaigns in which the British finally resolved the disputes

The five-hundred-foot façade of the Laxmi Vilas palace. The zenana *is on the right.*

149

An outsize bronze bull copied from an Italian sculpture.

The palace houses four inner courtyards. Here the palm trees have grown up above the level of the building itself.

A pan *or betel box made of gold and studded with rubies and diamonds.*

between the Peshwa, his generals and all the other aspirant princes of central and western India; the British, of course, resolved the disputes in their own favour, and decided that they should assume direct control of those parts of Gujarat which the Peshwa had claimed to control. But this still left the Gaekwads with one of the biggest, and one of the richest, princely states in India.

In the early nineteenth century the British found Baroda no more endearing than any of the other Maratha territories. There were minor revolts, stories of frightful maladministration, and plentiful evidence that the riches of eighteenth-century warfare and nineteenth-century agrarian prosperity were being diverted towards vain and sumptuous display – the Gaekwads boasted a diamond bigger than the Kohinoor, a carpet woven in pearls and diamonds, a pair of cannons cast from silver and a pair cast from gold. But with the accession of Sayajirao III in 1881, matters were very quickly transformed.

Italian marble was imported for the floor of the entrance hall.

The emblem of the Baroda family is the elephant. The one on the left guards the entrance to the Maharaja's apartments; the one on the right guards the entrance to the Maharani's apartments.

The transition can hardly have been expected. Sayajirao had been preceded by Malhar Rao, who had been so anxious to attain the throne that he had unsuccessfully attempted to poison his elder brother (with ground diamonds, of course), and had still been languishing in prison when his brother's natural death finally gave him the throne. That seat he occupied for only three years before he was suspected of another act of poisoning, again unsuccessful and this time directed against the British Resident; he was obliged to abdicate. Moreover, this messy scandal left the Baroda throne without an obvious heir and a distant relation was hauled out of a village and placed on it. Soon after he was presented to the Prince of Wales and despite the fact that he was young, un-prepared by his rural upbringing, and weighed down (literally) with the clutter of a profligate recent past, he made an immediate impression:

'All eyes were dazzled when Maharaja Syaji Rao stood at the threshold of the door; a crystallised rainbow. He is a small, delicately-framed lad for his twelve years and more, with a bright pleasant face. He was weighted – head, neck, chest and arms, fingers and ankles – with such a sight and wonder of vast diamonds, emeralds, rubies and pearls, as would be worth the loot of many a rich town.'

Another observer remarked that he 'appears to his inferiors every inch a king, as though he had sat on the *gadi* (throne) for half a century'.

Sayajirao took Baroda on a forced march from its feudal past towards a rich and elegant future. Roads and railways spread out across the state, a Department of Agriculture encouraged the production of cotton and other valuable crops in the good Gujarat soil, and Departments of Co-operation, Industry and Commerce added banks, a cotton industry and a variety of craft centres. The state prospered yet, according to Sayajirao, wealth was useless without enlightenment. Thus the riches of the Baroda treasury helped to found a system of free and compulsory education, and a fleet of mobile libraries, while the ruler outlawed bigamy and child marriages and encouraged many other social reforms. There were also dispensaries and hospitals, a modern legal system founded around new codes of law, and by the early twentieth century there was a Legislative Council and all the panoply of representative government. Meanwhile the Maharani pushed forward the cause of Indian women. She campaigned against the institution of *purdah*, chaired the first All India Women's Conference, and shot tigers with all the skill and enthusiasm of her spouse. In 1887 the Maharaja and Maharani visited Europe and were received by Queen Victoria at Windsor Castle.

The town of Baroda still had an old amphitheatre where fights were staged between buffaloes, rams or elephants. The palace kept a troupe of performing parrots which could ride bicycles and fire off cannons. The Maharaja bought a five-hundred-ton schooner, and Baroda had a state anthem arranged by Major R. Wood, the state's Director of Music.

Laxmi Vilas, a synthesis of Indian styles: a Moghul dome above the Bengal-inspired drooping canopies, Gujarati domes and towers, and a profusion of Rajput detail.

And of course Sayajirao built himself a palace. Until the 1860s the family still occupied the old Nazar Bagh palace, a tall building with an encrustation of pavilions and kiosks on the roof which the French traveller, Rousselet, found very disquieting: 'The mass of buildings, planted on the summit of an edifice almost entirely of wood, whose foundations were soaking in a damp soil, betokened great audacity on the part of the architects, and still more confidence on that of the king'. The inside was dark and cavernous, and Sayajirao felt it was better suited to act as a storehouse for the family jewels rather than as a residence. His new Laxmi Vilas was completed in 1890.

It had taken twelve years to build and had cost around £180,000. It was designed by Major Mant, who also designed palaces at Kolhapur and Darbhanga (his tragic career is mentioned in the Kolhapur chapter), but completed by Robert Fellowes Chisholm. As Chisholm told the Royal Institute of British Architects in 1896:

'It must be kept in view that the native Rajas and chiefs of India are passing through a transitional period; that an old palace like that at Ambur would be about as useless to the present Gaekwar of Baroda as to an ordinary English gentleman.'

Mant's design aimed to 'combine native detail with the ordinary requirements of a modern palace and arrangement of rooms'.

Thus Mant stuck more or less to the traditional arrangement of an Indian palace – with three distinct and separate parts for the public rooms, Maharaja's private apartments, and the ladies' quarters respectively – but incorporated many new rooms to suit the Baroda family's increasingly western life-style – stately dining rooms, billiard rooms, and great apartments for distinguished European visitors. Similarly, he attempted to incorporate the best elements of many periods of Indian architecture with some of the functional touches and decorative

A peacock urn made in Agra.

Maharaja Fatesinghrao Gaekwad of Baroda.

flourishes of different European schools. The sheer size of the palace (the frontage was over five hundred feet long) made it possible to include all these elements without creating stylistic havoc. Mant rejected from the start any idea of a dry symmetrical pattern, and allowed the styles to melt into one another. The exterior of the Maharaja's apartments were dressed up in the garb of Hindu martial architecture, with most of the detail borrowed from the fortress of Bharatpur. The public apartments, however, moved more into a Moghul style, while the ladies' quarters ended in a forest of domes and canopies copied from the Jain temples of Gujarat. However, even amongst this Indian *tour de force,* as Chisholm noted:

'In regard to detail an architect inspecting the forms critically will see evidence of European feeling in much of the ornament and massing of the forms. There is a thought of Venice in many of the arches, and a more decided feeling of Gothic in others, and towards the south end of the building a distinct leaning to an earlier and somewhat purer type of [classical European] art.'

Likewise the materials used were a blend of east and west. The basic construction was brick faced with red sandstone from the quarries of Agra, with some blue trapstone from Poona and marble from the quarries of Rajasthan. Workmen from Madras came to apply the *chunam* plaster to many of the interior walls. Then twelve workmen from the Murano Company of Venice spent eighteen months in Baroda laying the floor of Venetian mosaic in the Durbar hall. Carrara marble was imported for the doorways of the hall, the pillars and the ornamental staircase. Mr Tree from London made the moulding and gilding on the walls and ceilings, Mr Goldring from Kew laid out the gardens, Signor Felici from Italy made the sculptures which decorated the staircase, Durbar hall and other public rooms, and Mr Dix from London executed the stained glass windows. Period furniture, Old Masters and Venetian chandeliers completed the effect.

It is perhaps fitting that this concrete encyclopaedia of eastern and western architectural styles is probably on its way to becoming an Arts Centre. With its eclectic Indian exterior and lush European interior, it will serve as a characteristic monument to the memory of Sayajirao, and to the curious bridging role which the princes were obliged to play in the era of British rule.

*Vijay Vilas, an Indo-Edwardian pile
set among the sand-dunes of one of the
remotest stretches of western India.*

KUTCH

Kutch, the westernmost extremity of India, has a remoteness that cannot be explained merely by distance. It is all but cut off from the mainland either by the sea or by that geographical freak known as the Rann. This low-lying area to the north and east of Kutch (the Great and Little Ranns respectively) is inundated for five months of the year, and emerges for the rest of the time as a hard, salt-encrusted wasteland inhabited only by wild asses and countless flocks of flamingoes. On several occasions in the past, and most recently in 1819, earthquakes have redistributed the Rann, and gobbled up more of the usable territory. In the Rann, laments one writer, 'there is not a sign of vegetable life', and the Kutchis have always looked for sustenance to the sea.

It is said that Vasco da Gama saw Kutchi ships anchored at Mombasa and that he used a Kutchi pilot to guide him from Zanzibar to the Malabar coast. Certainly for centuries the Kutchis played a prominent part as sailors and merchants in the coasting trade that ranged from Zanzibar at one end, through the ports of Arabia, the Persian Gulf and peninsular India to Calcutta at the other. Zanzibar was particularly important as a trading partner and Kutchi ships brought ivory, cloves and rhinoceros hides from Africa in return for the cotton, rice, salt and pottery of India. The Moghuls dealt lightly with Kutch because the Kutchi navy served an important part of their strategy for controlling the western coast of India in the face of European commercial competition, and because the ports of Kutch were conveniently situated for the embarkation of pilgrims on their way to Mecca. There were eight hundred ships trading out of the port of Mandvi when the British arrived in 1819, the port dues yielded a revenue of a hundred thousand

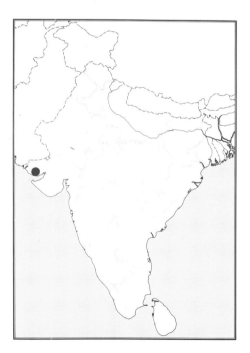

rupees a year, and the Muslim traders known as Kutchi Memoms had establishments 'in all the ports of Arabia and Africa'.

Considering their dependence on the sea it is not surprising that the rulers of Kutch made the port of Mandvi their second capital and studded it with palaces. The most famous, and curious, of these is the Old Palace built by Rao Lakhpat in the mid-eighteenth century. Its design owes everything to the extraordinary tale of Ram Singh the Navigator.

Ram Singh was a ship's boy from nearby Kathiawad who, in the early years of the eighteenth century, was shipwrecked off the coast of Africa and rescued by a Dutch ship on its way home to the Netherlands. In Europe he discovered that he had a remarkable talent for craft work and for the next eighteen years he stayed in Europe and learnt a whole range of industrial skills – tile-making, glass-blowing, clock-making, stone-carving, foundry work, building construction and, most of all, the enamel work in which the Dutch of the period had a special talent. He returned home hoping for patronage from the Kathiawad princes, but was disappointed to find that they had no use for his skills. Yet before long he finished up at a relative's house at Mandvi, and discovered that the merchants of Mandvi were more appreciative. Then the Raja of Kutch, Rao Lakhpat, got to hear of him, and Ram Singh was quickly taken under the umbrella of Kutchi royal patronage. Rao Lakhpat gave him a workshop in the palace, summoned all the best craftsmen in the state to act as his assistants and pupils, and sent him twice back to Europe to perfect his skills and to show his pupils the arts of the Netherlands, Venice and Austria. Thus, by the end of the eighteenth century this little state clinging to the edge of western India and threatened by a shifting salt desert was humming with the skills of industrial Europe. There was a glass factory, a tile workshop, an iron foundry manufacturing cannon, a workshop turning out clocks and watches on the European pattern, and an enamelling business which became famous throughout India.

A window carved like frozen lace.

Ram Singh the Navigator left his own memorial in the Old Palace at Mandvi. The façade of white stone is decorated with sculpted figures of gods, dancing-girls, elephants, flowers, alligators, cattle and the likenesses of the jolly, boozy Dutch apprentice-boys who taught Ram Singh his trade. All the figures have the detail, movement and naturalism of eighteenth-century Dutch art. Inside is the Aina Mahal, or Hall of Mirrors. The conception here is of course purely Indian, but the execution depended on Ram Singh's skills. He covered the white marble walls with mirrors and gilded ornaments of his own making, lined the floor with china tiles from his factory, designed a water system to deck the room with fountains, and lit the entire creation with hanging candelabra of Venetian glass. Amidst this sparkling array of ornament his patron, Rao Lakhpat, wrote poetry and watched his dancing-girls before retiring to his bedchamber which was crammed with the acquisitions of

*The Maharao is an enthusiastic
gardener and likes to sit here looking
out into his formal garden.*

Ram Singh's European trips – chiming clocks, globes, antique pictures,
mechanical toys, glass and china and even Hogarth cartoons.

It was a wonderful conception, but the cost broke Rao Lakhpat's
treasury. The Kutchi nobles rose in revolt, the British and Maratha
troops pressed on Kutch's borders, and the emphasis in Kutchi affairs
switched away from Mandvi and the sea and back to the fortified inland
capital of Bhuj.

This was not unusual as Kutch had as warlike a history as any other
Indian state. The ruling line were Rajputs who had come into Kutch
from Sind or northern India in the late fifteenth century, but had only
settled on the strategic rock of Bhuj as their capital in 1548 after a short
but bloody history of dynastic strife. However Bhuj suffered very little
from outside interference. The Moghuls even exempted Kutch from the
payment of tribute in return for a free passage for the Mecca pilgrims in
Kutchi ships, and the town of Bhuj was not properly fortified until the

The winter residence of the Maharao is an Italianate villa in Bhuj.

The Dutch façade built by Ram Singh the Navigator on the old palace at Mandvi.

time of troubles which marked the decline of Moghul power. In 1723 Rao Godji threw a wall thirty-five feet high and four feet thick around the town and equipped it with fifty-one guns. But in fact the major threat to the Kutchi rulers in this period came not from the world outside but from the Bhayad, or the hereditary nobles who built their own forts on every available knoll in Kutch, siphoned off the revenues which might have gone to the treasury and hemmed the ruler in on all sides. The ruler was powerless to prevent his more unruly subjects committing acts of piracy in the coastal waters and conducting looting raids in the territories of Kathiawad. Once the British had established treaties with the states in Kathiawad, and assumed general control of the coastal waters, they had an excuse to march into Kutch on the pretence of restoring order. Their real aim was to secure Kutch as a buffer state against the French in Sind. In the immediate aftermath of their action, which resulted in the deposition of the Kutchi prince and the destruction of Bhuj's fortifications, an earthquake shifted the Rann.

The affairs of the Kutchi ruling house festered in the early nineteenth century because the British mistook the notorious Bhayad for an assemblage of nobles along the lines of those who had besieged King John, wrote a treaty which could act as the Bhayad's Magna Charta, and tried to organise them into a parliament on the medieval model. The result was utter disorder, and the Kutchi princely rulers did not manage to rise above the fray until they could restore their independent income through fostering Mandvi's trade in the second half of the century. This was very much the work of Pragmalji, who ruled from 1860 to 1876. He improved the harbour at Mandvi, built roads and irrigation works, and used the increasing revenue from customs to build schools, a jail, courts, hospitals and new palaces. The most spectacular of these was the pink Italianate villa built on the outskirts of Bhuj and used for private entertaining. Soon, however, the emphasis shifted back to the more salubrious seaside town of Mandvi. The old Dutch palace had by now fallen into decay and was well on its way to being turned over for use as a girls' school. Thus the Maharaja chose a site outside the town, close to the sea, and in the 1920s built the new palace of Vijay Vilas. The architect and craftsmen were brought from Jaipur, and the result is a curious farrago of contemporary British and ancient oriental inspiration. The three-storeyed structure is built largely in the style of Indo-Saracenic architecture favoured on the official buildings of the empire by this stage of its history. Yet the appearance is strangely disrupted by *art nouveau* windows and by other touches of contemporary European style. The roof resembles the flat terrace of the colonial bungalow, but is then invaded by a collection of towers and domes which seems to have strayed south-west (and across several centuries) from Muslim Gujarat. Around the palace, a lush and spectacular garden has been coaxed out of the sandy and saline soil.

Vijay Vilas seen from the garden.

PORBANDAR

'It stands in the most magnificent position overlooking a lake with hills all round and a view over the plain towards the sea. In the monsoon, when it is all green, it must be like one of the Italian lakes.' Thus William Barton, a British official in the political service, recorded his visit to the Daria Rajmahal palace of Porbandar in Kathiawad at the turn of the century. Barton found the palace spectacular and unusual and thus in keeping with this remote corner of India. The Maharaja laid on an equally unusual entertainment for Barton which finished up with

'a traditional dance done by the men of one of the villages. It reminded me partly of Morris dances and partly of Russian steps with that typical squatting position on the heels and sudden leap-up. I had never seen anything like it before in India.'

In the days of sail Porbandar flourished. Local tradition identifies the city with the Sudampuri mentioned in the epic poem, the *Mahabharatha*, and through early modern times Porbandar traded with Africa and Arabia. Even more recently, Porbandar helped to embellish the richest quarters of Bombay and Karachi, the great port cities of the west of the subcontinent. The solid banks and business houses which the British set up in the main streets of these two cities, and the even more forbidding houses of the Parsi millionaires in the luxurious suburbs behind, were built of the creamy stone mined from the Barda hills on the westernmost point of the Kathiawad peninsula and exported through the port of Porbandar. But little stone is exported now, the port has decayed, and Murray's *Handbook* rightly calls Porbandar 'this very old-world corner'.

The rulers of Porbandar belong to a Rajput clan which, according to legend, once reigned in Kashmir. They have been in Kathiawad for two thousand years and originally ruled from the town of Morvi. At that time the Kathiawad peninsula was almost an island – it is only river-silt and earthquakes that have much more recently attached Kathiawad more firmly to the subcontinent. It also served as an island of refuge, constantly receiving new injections of population, generally in flight from the warfare of Sind or northern India. It was thus also a notoriously unstable region, famed for its fugitives and its robbers. The future ruling clan of Porbandar at times held sway over the whole peninsula, but at other times were themselves in flight and forced to move their capital ahead of their pursuers. Eventually they were forced back to Ghumli, a gloomy gorge in the Barda hills above Porbandar; here there are still ruins of twelfth-century temples.

From those days onwards the clan's history is recorded in the ballads composed by the professional court singers, called Bhats. These ballads remain popular. Two of the favourite subjects are the rulers Halaman and Nagarjoon. The tales of Halaman's reign combine warfare with romance in the classic fashion of the popular song, and in the nineteenth century the tales were transformed into a Gujarat play, *Halaman Jethva*.

The influence of Porbandar's trading connections with Arabia is evident in the Daria Rajmahal built on the shores of the Arabian Sea.

A carpet of velvet and silver thread adorns the throne room in the Anut Nivas Khambala palace.

It is still performed and was most recently republished in 1960. Meanwhile the other hero, Nagarjoon, was depicted as so fierce in battle that his body fought on and slaughtered many enemies even after it had been separated from Nagarjoon's head. He is also depicted as a miracle-worker with a flair for alchemy who 'transformed the fort of Dhank from stone to gold'.

The ripples set off by the Moghul invasion of northern India propelled a new wave of refugees into the Kathiawad peninsula in the sixteenth century and set off a new period of warfare and pillage which ultimately pushed the clan right back to the sea. In 1785 the family finally settled at Porbandar. By this time its catalogue of tributary obligations reflected how easily the clan had fallen prey to its stronger military neighbours and been forced to buy a measure of independence at quite a high price: the Porbandar state paid tribute to the neighbouring chiefs of Banton and Mangrole, to the Nawab of Junagadh in the south of Kathiawad, to

The sea frontage of the Daria Rajmahal Khambhala built in 1927.

the Maratha generals who commanded access to the peninsula, to the pirate bands who patrolled the Kathiawad coast, and to the Portuguese traders in their nearby settlement at Diu. Thus it was with a certain resignation, and even some optimism, that in 1807 the ruler of Porbandar accepted the overlordship of the British East India Company.

Maharaja Bhavsinhji built the palace Daria Rajmahal at the turn of this century. It was designed by the state's engineer, Phulchand Parekh, and naturally enough it was built of Porbandar stone. It was sited right on the water's edge looking out into the Arabian Sea and indeed the design seems more Arab than Indian. This is hardly surprising since the Arab sailing-ships had been calling in Kathiawad since the eighth century, and there had often been settlements of Arab merchants in the ports of the peninsula. In the eighteenth century, Porbandar had been ringed around by a great fortified wall with five gates guarded by Arab soldiers. Most of the chiefs of Kathiawad kept bands of armed retainers who were

The marble fountain in the main reception room of the Anut Nivas Khambala.

recruited from the coastline of Arabia, Persia and Sind and brought to their new homes by the ships of the coastal trade. The three storeys of balconies ringing a central courtyard in the Daria Rajmahal recall the *serais* built by the Arab merchants in all the stopping places along their trade routes.

But in detail the Daria Rajmahal is most like an Italian country villa. There is a blend of Gothic and Renaissance features which very closely follows the transitional style popular in north Italy in the early sixteenth century and which was revived in the nineteenth century and then termed 'Venetian'. The quatrefoil windows and fountain and the rather heavy, pedimented façade of the two wings are clearly late-Gothic in inspiration, while the colonnaded courtyard, and the tiers of varying pillared arches in the main part of the building are close copies of the early Venetian Renaissance. These influences had not of course come on the coastal trade routes of the Indian Ocean but reflected the craze for Italianate design which had swept through the mansions of Europe and was now making its way into the palaces and town houses of India.

Inside Daria Rajmahal, however, there were all the usual rooms of an Indian palace, but again the details of ornament had been significantly altered in homage to European arts and crafts. The Durbar hall was decorated with paintings of Indian rural scenes, but in the form of oil paintings rather than the usual frescoes on the walls. The lighting of the hall relied on the same principle of dazzling chaos represented by the Sheesh Mahal or hall of mirrors in most palaces; but here the agent was not a ceiling crammed with mirror-work but an array of chandeliers shaped like umbrellas and festooned with crystal balls hung in clusters like bunches of grapes.

Like most of the princely families, Porbandar had a chief administrator or Dewan. For a time, one Uttamchand Gandhi held this post and, since such offices quite often became hereditary, passed it on to his two sons, Karamchand and Tulsidas, who held the office in turn. Karamchand later went off to serve as Dewan in other states. Before he left, however, his fourth wife bore him a son who was named Mohandas Karamchand – although posterity has generally edged out those forenames and replaced them with the title Mahatma, or great soul. The house where the leader of the Indian nationalist movement and apostle of non-violence was born in Porbandar is now a place of pilgrimage, the relatively humble residence surrounded by a cloister.

Bhavsinhji built not only the Daria Rajmahal palace but also roads and bridges, a town hall and library, a lake which improved irrigation throughout the state and a weir 'which transformed a vast tract of barren salt marshes into a fertile granary'. His successor Natwarsinhji took the state on a more rapid march to modernity. He found Daria Rajmahal too grandiose for his tastes, consigned it for use as a teacher training college, and in 1927 designed and built the new palace called Anut Nivas Khambala. It is a two-storeyed building with a formal garden on the edge of the sea and a reception hall with a fountain in the middle. There is a Rajput Room which acts as a museum of Kathiawad's past and a well-stocked library of Gujarati books, for Natwarsinhji took a lively interest in the resurgence of local art and literature which accompanied the growth of the nationalist movement and which was particularly strong in Gujarat. He composed music, exhibited paintings and wrote several books. The palace was his own design and although he stated that it 'is of no particular style', it resembles nothing quite so much as an enormous cricket pavilion. Again this is appropriate, for Natwarsinhji distinguished himself in all sports at Rajkot College, and in 1931 captained the first official Indian cricket team in England.

A silver cradle lined in scarlet brocade and equipped with a silver rattle and silver bells. It was made at the time of the present Maharaja's birth in 1900.

MORVI

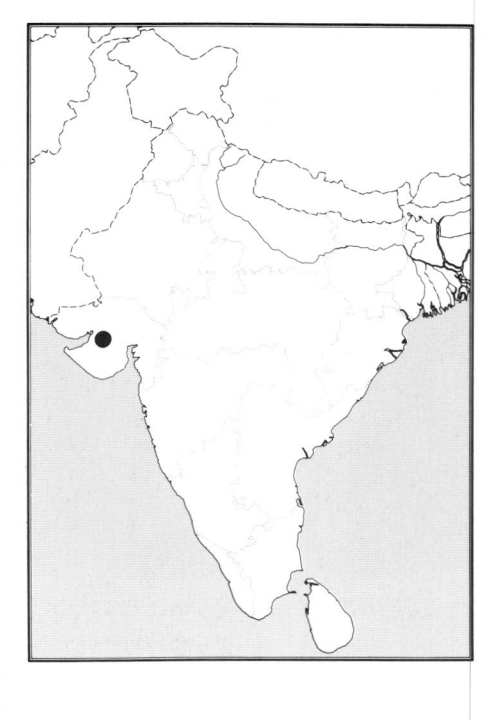

The peninsula of Kathiawad has always been rich and vulnerable. The riches come from both the land and the sea. The warm, well-watered interior supports a flourishing agriculture, and the ports that dot the long seaboard have long traded with Arabia and Africa. This seemingly remote little territory has participated remarkably fully in the making of north India's history and mythology. Krishna is supposed to have reigned and died here, and the ancient Buddhist Emperor Ashoka left his edicts inscribed on a rock. But from medieval times onwards the peninsula has acted as a dangerously vulnerable cul-de-sac. The Rajput tribes who fled here after the Muslim invasions of the Punjab found that they were easily hemmed in by whatever power commanded the narrow neck of land which joined the peninsula to Gujarat and the rest of India beyond. The Moghul rulers in Ahmedebad, then the Maratha armies, and finally the British government stood across this landward gateway, extracted a tribute from the peninsula's population, and thereafter left well alone.

The result has been a rather suffocating history. The premier Rajput families in Kutch and Kathiawad were among the very few in India who practised infanticide. Some still continued to do so until well into the nineteenth century. These families found it so difficult to find suitable matches for their children, particularly once the Muslim power had cut them off from the Rajput families of central India, that infanticide became the only alternative to either horrific in-breeding or unseemly dilution of the royal blood.

Infanticide went hand in hand with internecine strife, and indeed the state of Morvi was born out of the rivalries within the neighbouring ruling house of Kutch. The difficulties began in the late seventeenth century when the Rao of Kutch bestowed the principality of Morvi on a favourite son, Rangji. This was a somewhat careless act, since the territory of Morvi commanded the access to the virtual island of Kutch; the Rao seems temporarily to have forgotten that his own forebears had originally captured the Kutchi throne by commanding Morvi and then using this bridgehead to squeeze out the current incumbent of the throne. However, the indulgent father clearly thought Rangji was to be trusted. Rangji's younger brother, Pragji, was not. He assassinated Rangji, usurped the throne of Morvi, and then repeated history by using the control of Morvi to besiege Kutch and finally displace his father from the throne. There matters did not end because Rangji's son raised an army, defeated his nefarious uncle in battle and placed him under arrest. The two kinsmen however then came to an agreement: the chastened Pragji was restored to the throne of Kutch, while the victorious nephew decided to hang on to the strategic principality of Morvi.

The same sort of cloistered quarrelling had fragmented Kathiawad into a mass of little states, and because the British seemed no more interested than the Moghuls and Marathas before them in exercising

The suspension bridge to the old Dubargadh Waghaji palace was built in 1882. Servants had to take off their shoes when walking across. The bridge was badly damaged in the floods of 1979.

direct rule in this little nook of western India, all these states were confirmed by a treaty in 1807. Within the 22,000 square miles of the peninsula there were no fewer than two hundred and twenty-two separate states. The smallest of these had no more than a quarter of a square mile and a couple of hundred inhabitants, and some which were hardly any bigger were internally subdivided amongst members of the 'ruling' family, who feuded with all the zest of many of the truly 'princely' houses. Moreover, these tiny territories were so hopelessly intertwined that there was a mass of enclaves and fragmented principalities. Several of these little units insisted on operating their own customs systems, which made internal trade a nightmare, and smuggling a well-organised business. The populations of several of these states contained a large number of criminal offenders in flight from justice in the neighbouring territories. Smuggling and moonlighting made Kathiawad famous for its bandits.

'The Catti,' wrote Colonel Tod, referring to the people of Kathiawad, 'still adores the sun, scorns the peaceful arts and is much less contented with the tranquil subsistence of industry than the precarious earnings of his former predatory pursuits.' Morvi was constantly being invaded. Inside the palace, too, the feuds continued. When the Morvi ruler's son was sent to school in the late nineteenth century 'soldiers guarded the college corridors every night, and armed sentries stood round the cricket field, because an intimation had been received that an attempt would be made to carry off the young chief of Morvi'.

This well-protected schoolboy went on to become Morvi's last and most remarkable ruler. His father had laid the basis for his success by abolishing infanticide and thus ingratiating himself with the British overlords, and by digging enough wells to 'banish famine for ever'. The son, Waghji, mounted the throne in 1879 and remained there until 1948. In this reign Morvi emerged as a prosperous and comfortable

little city-state. Waghji built the usual roads and railways, and also seven hundred miles of tramway which joined Morvi to the inland state of Wadhwan. He also touched up the two trim little ports of Vavania and Navlakha so that they could take small ocean-going vessels and could export the state's production of salt and cloth. He then combined his strictly feudal and personal rule with an extensive involvement in local commerce. The ruling house grew rich, but also the people's taxes dwindled away. Waghji posed as a benevolent godfather to his ninety thousand subjects.

He combined munificence with a ruthless firmness. The professional bandits were pursued back to their lairs; policemen had their salaries docked if they failed to catch criminals. No newspaper was allowed to appear, and no-one was permitted to speak his mind too loudly in public. On top of this, Waghji also kept a firm hand on the economy: he allowed no banks or moneylenders to operate in his territory, and

Stone balustrades line a promenade around the roof of the palace. The dome is an unusual modern treatment of a traditional design.

The new palace built between 1931 and 1944.

The interior of the new palace was designed in the style of late art deco. This arch and fountain stand in the courtyard.

174

instead Waghji himself loaned money at low interest to the state's commercial enterprises.

One of Waghji's first acts was to equip his little city-state with a suitable palace. Beside the river running through his capital he placed a Venetian Gothic mansion. Even though a classical balustrade and some oriental flourishes intrude into the design, the riverside façade is really a remarkably faithful replication right down to the double *loggia* and the giant 'sea-door' through which the Venetian merchants took their goods right into the interior of the mansion. Inside, however, the Italianate courtyards have to co-exist with Saracenic domes, the Gothic windows have been surrounded by cusped Rajput arches, and the classical urns and balustrades mingle with Moghul kiosks.

Waghji had by 1948 become completely identified with his little city-state. He was its ruler, manager, patron and policeman. He could see the logical necessity of merging his principality into the emergent

A marble sunken bath.

The *new palace houses six dining rooms.*

The art deco *bar room is decorated with erotic murals.*

The *homage to* art deco *extended to the bedroom furniture.*

Cloister and fountain in the main courtyard.

independent country of India, but he could not bear to do it himself. Just days before the merger he arranged to pass Morvi over to his son.

Lakhdiraj thus officially ruled the state of Morvi for a handful of days. He had however gradually taken on more and more responsibility as his father had grown older and had already built a new palace. This building, appropriately enough, owes little to European design but rather belongs to a style which became increasingly popular after Independence. Many of the lesser official buildings in New Delhi and in the regional capitals of India share its rather clean, functional and unimaginative appearance. It belongs in inspiration firmly to the age of pre-stressed concrete rather than to the age of dressed stone, even though it is in fact constructed of the local granite. Inside, however, princely India is having its last fling. Six drawing rooms, six dining rooms and fourteen bedrooms jostle for space with a swimming pool, cardroom, billiard room and bar. Most of the rooms are designed and decorated in a pure *art deco* style, even down to such details as tubular-framed furniture. Lifts descend to a subterranean bedroom decorated with erotic murals, and a bathroom made up of sea-shells.

WANKANER

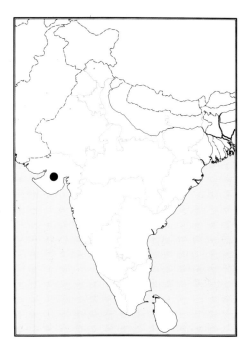

While Mahatma Gandhi was born in the state of Porbandar he spent some of his childhood in the state of Wankaner, for his father lost the post of Dewan or chief administrator in Porbandar as a result of political intrigues, and went on to serve as Dewan in Wankaner. He thus passed from the flat coastline of the Kathiawad peninsula to the hills in the centre of this unusual little territory which clings to the western shoulder of India. He was still, however, serving a Rajput prince, for the house of Wankaner derived from another band of Rajput warriors who had arrived in Kathiawad in flight from the troubles of northern India.

It is a familiar history of war, feuding, flight and changing fortunes. The annals of the Jhala Rajputs who eventually settled in Wankaner stretch back to a twelfth-century chieftain who commanded a handful of villages, built a castle, and began warring with his neighbours. Although the Kathiawad chiefs were operating on a rather smaller scale compared to their more illustrious cousins in Rajasthan, they nevertheless showed the same attachment to the Rajput traditions of chivalry, revenge and clan fidelity. Sometimes these values could lead them astray. In 1475 the Jhala chief returned to his capital and found that all the clan's womenfolk, who had seen the standard-bearer of the Jhala forces slain, had presumed the battle was lost and had immediately consigned themselves to the *johar*, the act of ritual immolation by the women of the clan which prevented the victorious rivals despoiling the honour of the Rajput warriors' women.

Somehow the Jhala clan survived this disaster, but the arrival of a Muslim ruler in the state of Gujarat, which straddled the access from the Kathiawad peninsula to the rest of India, made the Jhala chiefs flee their capital and become fugitives in the hills. Supposedly they eventually regained their capital by entering the Sultan of Gujarat's armed camp at night, seizing the Sultan by the throat as he lay asleep amidst his women, and demanding that he return their capital and territories.

By the end of the seventeenth century matters had settled down and a Jhala prince married one daughter of the Rajput house of Jodhpur at the same time that the future Moghul Emperor, Jahangir, married another. Now the Jhala clan did not seem to mind that it would count Muslims amongst its in-laws but there was still a quarrel over the exact order in which the marriages would take place, and the quarrel ended in the foundation of the state of Wankaner: in the short term the quarrel seemed to be settled in an amicable fashion for the two bridegrooms agreed to decide the order of precedence through a competition of horsemanship. But the Jhala chief won and to a man who would shortly become the Great Moghul and take a title which meant 'lord of the world' that was a little unbecoming. Some years later Jahangir turned on the Jhala Rajputs and banished the sons of his equestrian rival from their capital at Halvad. One exiled son, Sartanji, moved some forty miles to the south and established the principality of Wankaner.

The Ranjit Vilas palace built between 1907 and 1914 by the state engineer.

He, of course, tried to regain the old territories, feuded with the step-brother whom Jahangir had put in his rightful place, and even vowed not to go through a proper marriage ceremony until the old capital had been regained. Since it never was, except for a brief interval of four years, the rulers of Wankaner still undergo only a curiously truncated form of marriage ceremony.

In 1782 the family acquired another curious custom. The death of the Wankaner ruler occasioned the sort of palace intrigue which the Rajput princes had turned into a speciality. The rightful heir, Kesarsinhji, was careless enough to leave the fort and palace to attend the late ruler's funeral, and predictably enough while he was away his younger brother seized the fort and assumed the throne. Kesarsinhji later fought his way back in, but on future occasions the heir apparent was always kept carefully inside the palace during a time of royal succession.

The palace from the garden.

The centrepiece of the palace is a marble
spiral staircase with two sets of flights,
built so that those ascending are
screened off from those descending.

Once the state of Wankaner was firmly established, their main problem came from their warlike neighbours and from the many bandits who aimed to found, or usurp, a little principality just like that of Wankaner. In the late eighteenth century the rulers built a wall around their capital, fought back the bandits and neighbours, and made settlements with their vassals and feudatories. Thus in 1807 Wankaner was one of the many little Kathiawad states which had survived the obstacle race of Rajput history and which now were guaranteed by the power of the East India Company.

For the last sixty-seven years before Wankaner and the other states of Kathiawad were, in 1948, absorbed into the Indian Union, the ruler was Maharaja Amarsinhji. He had travelled widely, seen active service in France during the First World War, and worked to turn his principality into a rich little city-state. He also built the Ranjit Vilas palace which stands on a hill overlooking the town. It took seven years, was completed

Purna Chandra Bhavan, or Full Moon House, was once the royal guest-house and is now a hotel.

in 1914 and was designed by the Maharaja himself. The grounds around the palace extended to two hundred and twenty-five acres and also included the state guest house known as Chandra Bhavan, or Full Moon House. As architecture, Ranjit Vilas is a brave synthesis of styles. Arcades of arched windows borrowed from a Victorian conservatory lead up, with the help of some Italianate pillars, Gothic arches and classical parapets, to a Dutch roof surmounted by a couple of Moghul pavilions and a pair of domed kiosks which dither between the art of the Jaipur palace and the ambitions of Sir Christopher Wren. The whole is dominated by a clocktower which attempts to reiterate the whole pattern laid out below and is itself crowded with columns, parapets, kiosks and domes. Inside, a strong double staircase with classical balustrades and some ornamental Grecian urns winds down under cusped arches in the Rajput style past Venetian mosaics, Moghul inlay, ornamental elephant tusks and Romanesque barley-sugar pillars.

But Wankaner, and the Kathiawad peninsula generally, is littered with monuments that are smaller but even more arresting than Amarsinhji's palace. These are the lines of tombstone-like *pallias* which are a unique testament to Kathiawad's lawless past. These stones preserve the memory of a death or an act of bravery. The upper part of the stone has carvings of the sun and moon which record the date of the event, and the lower part has an image of the hero or heroine – on a horse if it was a man and in a chariot if a woman. Some of them have an image of an arm and hand, and this commemorates an act of *suttee*. The dwellers of Kathiawad were especially keen on *suttee* to the extent that it was not only women who sacrificed themselves in the wake of their husbands, but also mothers following their children, men following their wives, and even women for no apparent reason. Sir Alexander Walker, who visited Kathiawad in 1805, watched one woman immolate herself while her husband looked on and 'complained to me of the circumstance, not

One of the silver lion thrones made for Raj Pratap Singhji in the early twentieth century.

from feeling regret for his loss, but for the expense he was exposed to in his endeavours to procure another wife'. Most of the *pallias* however record the deaths of the Bhats or Charuns. These were poets and bards who were patronised by the princes and nobles of Kathiawad, and who also served both as warriors and, in a curious fashion, as sureties. Property was hardly secure in a region where robbery and piracy were endemic and so the local bankers were not impressed when a man offered some property as a pledge against a loan. Instead, the nobles and merchants who borrowed money put up their bards as the surety. If the debtor failed to repay the loan, the bard would be forfeit and would kill himself. This can hardly have been of much satisfaction to the moneylender, but it was such a blot on the honour of the borrower that it presumably acted as quite a deterrent to default. Many of the *pallias* carry the image of a mounted bard brandishing a spear in readiness for his act of suicide in the role of surety.

PATIALA

From the eighth century onwards the Hindu peoples of the Punjab witnessed the marches, countermarches and depredations of the Muslim armies which came down from the hills of Afghanistan and the plains of Persia and central Asia to take loot or found empires in the rich lands of northern India. Many Punjabis fell into line with the religion of the invading troops, and at the turn of the century an intense young intellectual, Nanak Chand, set out to discover for himself what were the best attributes of the two separate religions, Hinduism and Islam, which dominated his homeland. In the tradition of many Indian seekers after truth, he renounced family life and wandered widely throughout India and the Middle East; some say he even went to Mecca. He eventually returned to the Punjab and preached that God was infinite and indivisible, caste and idolatry were wrong, all men were brothers and all religions merited respect. Soon after his death, his followers were harassed by the Muslim rulers for belonging to an unorthodox sect, but they maintained Nanak's teaching through a succession of teachers, known as 'Gurus'. Gradually the persecution of the rulers transformed the rather metaphysically oriented sect into a defensive, warlike brotherhood. The bigoted Moghul Emperor, Aurangzeb, executed the ninth of the *gurus* and in the aftermath the tenth, Guru Gobind Singh, completed the transformation of Nanak's peaceful and eclectic creed into a strict and powerful dogma. Gobind Singh also added to the military aspect of the sect by prescribing a uniform equipped with martial symbols, and declared that no more *gurus* or teachers were necessary but in future the sectarians would have to organise and fight for their very existence. The most distinctive features of Guru Gobind Singh's uniform resulted from the demand that the hair should remain uncut; the huge black beard, and the large bright turbans to contain the long hair, are still the most distinctive marks of the followers of Sikhism.

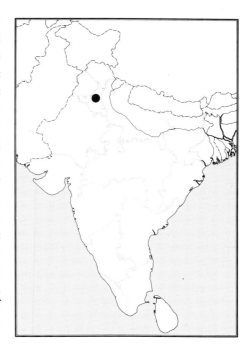

In the late eighteenth century the Sikhs organised themselves into twelve fierce militias, known as the *misls,* and drove the Moghuls from the Punjab. At the turn of the century Ranjit Singh bludgeoned the *misls* into a relatively unified state and made a treaty with the British which set the river Sutlej as the boundary between their respective domains. In 1830 Ranjit Singh died, his state fell apart, and the British marched in. In the fighting the British gained such respect for Sikh valour that once the Punjab had been finally pacified in 1848, the Sikhs were quickly drafted into the British Indian Army. But all the old Sikh leaders were relieved of their states, except those which had fallen on the 'British' side of the Sutlej river and been guaranteed by the treaty of 1848.

Patiala was the biggest of these Sikh states, and indeed everything about its history seems rather excessive. The ancestry of the Patiala family stretches back to a revenue official in the Moghul Empire,

Portrait by Simon Elwes of the late Maharaja Yadavindra Singh in his coronation regalia. An enormous cabochon emerald adorns the buckle of the belt.

The Old Motibagh palace, one of the largest residences in Asia.

further back to an offshoot from the Rajput ruling family of the desert kingdom of Jaisalmer, and even further (and a bit hazily) back to the founder of the Afghan town of Ghazni. In the sixteenth century the family was counted among the early adherents of the new Sikh faith, while a seventeenth-century letter from the tenth and last *guru*, Gobind Singh, is one of the family's most treasured relics. In the eighteenth century Baba Ala Singh led one of the twelve Sikh *misls* and founded his own kingdom at Patiala in 1752.

But after this initial history of religious and military service the family fell prey to another form of excess which was not uncommon among the warrior Punjabis. Two generations of Baba Ala's successors drank themselves into early graves. Baba Ala's grandson was the one man to avoid this curse and he made Patiala the most powerful state in the tract between the Jamuna and Sutlej rivers; but the survival of Patiala in the turmoil at the very end of the eighteenth century owed more to its womenfolk than to its men. The weakling Sahib Singh was helped through this difficult period firstly by his grandmother, Rani Hukman; secondly by his cousin, Rani Rajondar, who raised an army, invaded the state to settle the disputes which followed on from Rani Hukman's death and who then took this army out to keep the Maratha invaders at bay; and thirdly by his sister, Bibi Sahib Kaur, who took out the Patiala army to rout the Maratha invaders in 1794. Sahib Singh's successor was little better, and in his time the affairs of Patiala were managed by his wife.

The state had shrunk considerably by the time it came under British guarantee, but gradually through the nineteenth century it regained its strength and its reputation. The Patiala troops served the British during the Mutiny and the Afghan wars, and 37,000 of them went to fight in Mesopotamia, Aden and Gallipoli in the First World War. Moreover, in the 1870s Patiala began to enjoy the benefits of the lattice of irrigation canals which the British built across the Punjab. The wealth of the state increased and so did the stature of the ruling family. With the reign of Bhupinder Singh they both reached gargantuan proportions.

Bhupinder Singh did very little on a reasonable scale. He liked animals and birds and so he acquired a private zoo for himself. He enjoyed music and cricket, and so he maintained a private orchestra and a private cricket team. He liked jewels and appeared at one Viceregal Ball in Delhi in 1924 in 'a brocaded coat entirely concealed by diamonds' and made sure he became the owner of a necklace that had once belonged to the Empress Eugénie of France. He liked food and disturbed one British official by sitting down to tea and demolishing three whole chickens while his guest sipped nervously at his cup. He liked mischief so he

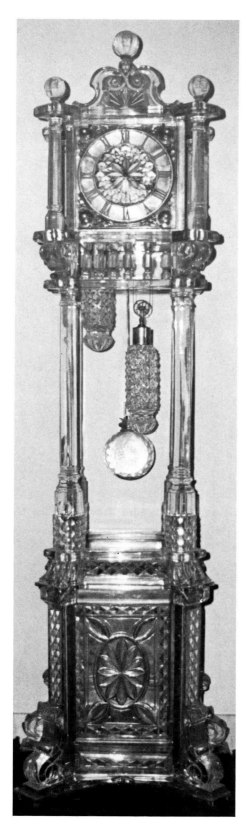

conducted a running feud with the Viceroy, Lord Willingdon, and kept signed portraits of Hitler and Mussolini on his mantelpiece to discomfort his European official guests. He liked his religion and lavished patronage on Sikh schools, Sikh scholars and the Punjab University. He liked entertaining so he threw enormous functions at which the guests overflowed even from the numerous and enormous rooms of his Motibagh palace and its annexes and camped out in the lawns and gardens. He liked pedigree dogs and purchased them not singly but in scores. He liked cars and so he had seventy-two, and he especially liked Rolls-Royces, so he made sure that three dozen of them were Rolls.

The palace had been constructed by his predecessor but it suited Bhupinder Singh's somewhat inflated taste. From the beginning it was reckoned to be one of the largest residences in Asia.

'The eleven acres of palace', the gushing popular author Maud Diver called it, 'an immensity of rose-pink sandstone that would make Versailles look like a cottage, the interminable façade soaring aloft from redder terraces, the vast central saloon furnished with English chairs and sofas, decorated chiefly with photographs of European royalties in jewelled frames; three generations of English kings set in isolated dignity on the piano; bedrooms like reception halls, the bathrooms like ballrooms.'

Sited in the middle of a huge and elaborate garden, the old Motibagh palace is an architectural wedding cake of mixed Rajput and Moghul concoction, frosted over with layers of Victorian icing. The colossal Durbar hall was hung with a hundred enormous chandeliers, and the fifteen dining rooms provided work for one hundred and forty-three cooks. Outside the main building there was also the Sheesh Mahal or hall of mirrors, which housed the senior ladies of the family, and the Baradari or Dozen Doors, which was a smaller, white marble pleasure-palace sited in a walled Moghul garden and furnished, according to one European visitor, with 'an enchanting collection of inherited chaos'.

It may have been an enormous palace but Bhupinder Singh found that he needed more space. For his greatest like – and it is clear that he did not care to leave his desires unfulfilled – was women. Even up to his death in 1938 Bhupinder Singh continued to accumulate wives by a procedure which was not unlike the *droit de seigneur*, and a large part of the Motibagh complex was occupied by them and their children. After the Mutiny the British bestowed on the Patiala family the title 'Favoured Son of the British Empire' and Bhupinder Singh seems to have considered it an act of special loyalty to find for the Empire as many 'grandchildren' as possible. One estimate put the total at eighty-seven, and one visiting English lady was a little shocked when it was explained that a parade of six perambulators which passed along the Motibagh verandah as she was taking tea contained merely the Maharaja's offspring born in a recent week. Bhupinder Singh's feudal excesses provoked quite a

The New Motibagh built in 1959 amidst a formal garden.

Yadavindra Singh was a renowned horticulturalist. Besides this impressive cactus garden he also grew grapes for wine.

storm in the 1920s, but in his own terms he had a defence close at hand: his subjects considered it was especially fortunate just to gaze on a son of the Maharaja, and the Maharaja was clearly doing his best to improve his subjects' chances of acquiring such good fortune.

After Independence, the Patiala family was still prominent. Maharaja Yadavindra Singh headed Sikh religious foundations, presided over the All India Sports Council, represented India at the United Nations, and served as an Ambassador to Rome and The Hague. He also built a new Motibagh palace and though this building was rather more restrained than its predecessor it still contained two acres of carpet. The valuable mementoes of the family were all moved to the new residence, so that now in Old Motibagh, where in 1938 hundreds of women lamented and wailed on the death of Bhupinder Singh, the men of the National Institute of Sports, a sort of finishing school for India's athletes and sportsmen, clatter incongruously around the echoing halls and galleries.

KAPURTHALA

Travelling up from Delhi through the hot, flat and rich countryside of the Punjab you pass through innumerable towns and villages in which the faded brick houses seem to have been caught in a web created by a maddened spider spinning electric cable. The dusty main street is filled with a mass of bicycles, and every male face seems to have the great black beard and the gay turban of the Sikh. At the end of the street, you plunge back into the seemingly endless fields of wheat. You could go on all the way through this rich, lively but repetitive landscape until you reach Kashmir or Pakistan. But if you detour through Kapurthala you suddenly run into royalist France.

Indeed you could be forgiven for thinking that you had suddenly fetched up at Fontainebleau itself. It is not only the Maharaja of Kapurthala's palace that is a remarkably faithful act of homage to Louis XIV, but also the town that spreads out around. 'There are some delicious pink villas,' noted one English visitor earlier this century, 'to which

one can imagine the Parisian *bourgeois* retiring in middle age.' She added with all the national pride and horticultural arrogance of a lady of the Empire: 'The gardens of these are as neat and as unimaginative as their prototypes in the suburbs of Fontainebleau.'

There was no premonition that, at the end of the nineteenth century, the successors of one of the leading Sikh warrior princes should start to revive Louis XIV with such studied effect. Back in the eighteenth century Sardar Jassa Singh was a leader of another of the Sikh militias or *misls*. Between 1747 and his death in 1783 he carved one state out of the chaos of the Punjab, lost it to the rival *misl* of the Patiala rulers, and so turned against the old Moghul commander of the Punjab, turfed him out of his fort at Kapurthala, and set up a second state. His successors inherited one of the biggest warrior-states in the Punjab and Fateh Singh of Kapurthala was co-signatory with the great Sikh leader, Ranjit Singh, at the treaty made with the British in 1808. But the

The Jagajit palace, inspired by Versailles and built between 1900 and 1908.

193

Rococo gilded ceiling in the French salon.

Lapis Lazuli columns imported from Italy.

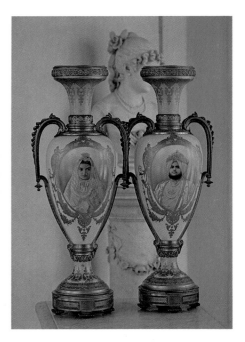

Sèvres porcelain and ormolu vases bearing the portraits of Maharaja Jagatjit Singh and his Maharani.

expansion of Jassa Singh and the treaty signed in 1808 laid the basis for future problems. Jassa Singh had acquired lands both to the north and to the south of the Sutlej river and now the treaty of 1808 stipulated that the Sutlej should form the boundary between the East India Company's territory and Ranjit Singh's emergent Sikh kingdom. The Kapurthala rulers would have liked to remain as independent as they were in the freebooting days of the eighteenth century but they could not really evade overlordship by one of the two powers which were consolidating themselves in the Punjab. The question was: which side to join?

The Kapurthala rulers vacillated, and nearly lost everything. Fateh Singh had 'exchanged turbans' as a mark of brotherhood with Ranjit Singh and so at first he placed his southern estates at risk and served as a leading lieutenant in Ranjit Singh's campaigns. But as he watched Ranjit Singh methodically crushing out the other Sikh principalities and merging them into his own Sikh kingdom, he began to feel he had made the wrong choice. In 1825 he suddenly fled across the Sutlej, abandoned his estates to the north, and appealed to the British for protection. The British were not impressed and Fateh Singh returned to Kapurthala to live out a rather sulky retirement. Then in 1845, his successor Nihal Singh was so uncertain which side to back in the war between the British and the late Ranjit Singh's kingdom, that he kept firmly and tacitly within the bounds of his own fort and allowed his own troops to do whatever they liked. Since his troops inevitably backed the Sikh forces, at the end of the war the British seized Kapurthala's southern portions. There was now not much of the Kapurthala principality left and in the next decades the rulers made sure they retained that: they gave definite help to the British both in the second Sikh war and in the Mutiny of 1857, and were rewarded with titles, territory and security.

The subsequent rulers of Kapurthala set out to turn their little

Empire-style table with Italian mosaic.

Louis-Quatorze furniture imported from France.

principality, sited in the midst of some of the richest agricultural land in northern India, into a model city-state. The most remarkable transformation fell in the reign of Jagatjit Singh who came to the throne in 1890. His long minority had coincided with the period when the British became intensely interested in the education of India's princely rulers. Jagatjit's English tutors had taught him flawless English and French and taken him on tours of Europe. He was completely captivated by France, the French, French food and the style of Louis XIV. He returned and started turning his little city-state into 'a scrap of Paris laid at the foot of the Himalayas'.

To begin with, his new palace and gardens had to be modelled on Versailles. He hired a French architect, M. Marcel, and entitled the project, rather inevitably, the Elysée palace. The original plans turned out to be rather optimistic and the building which started out with red sandstone had to be finished off with pink plaster to save money. But in other ways it was suitably extravagant. M. Marcel belonged to the *beaux arts* school which was so popular in late nineteenth-century France. The central section of his Kapurthala Elysée palace was remarkably like a pavilion-end from Fontainebleau. The Mansard roof with its *oeil-de-boeuf* windows were copied from the Paris Louvre, as were the coupled columns lining the blind arcade on the two wings. Inside, the royalist illusion continued. It was, according to one dazzled European visitor, 'one mass of gold with nymphs disporting themselves on vaulted ceilings and innumerable Sèvres ornaments and vases and *objets d'art* about'. Lapis Lazuli pillars had been brought over from Italy, marble for the fireplaces had come from Carrara, and Aubusson carpets had been specially woven to fit the rooms. Artists had been imported to paint the ceilings of the principal rooms, while plaster mouldings and gold paint ran riot through the halls and corridors.

At the time of building, many of the great houses of Paris were

*Detail of one of
the Gobelin tapestries.*

being knocked down to make way for the boulevards and it was easy to secure furniture and ornamentation to suit the palace's design. Most of the furniture came from France, and the main reception hall was named the Louis XIV room in honour of the project's spiritual mentor. The gardens were strewn with stone staircases, fountains, parapets and statuary in the style of a French mansion. Jagatjit Singh's devotion to France, which he visited many times, was eventually rewarded with the Grand Cross of the Légion d'Honneur.

The Maharaja extended his Gallic influence to the rest of his little city-state, and thus the environs of the palace took on the appearance of a French suburb. But not all the building was simply pursued in a spirit of luxury: beside the palace and the villas stood a prison, law-courts, school, hospital, post office and co-operative credit bank all with 'the charming appearance of being planned for an exhibition of decorative art'. Many distinguished visitors passed through to view this anoma-

Marble fountain.

Villa Buona Vista, a shooting-lodge completed in 1894.

lous little principality, largely because the Maharaja kept his chefs well trained in French cooking and thereby gained a reputation as one of the most attractive hosts in northern India.

The Elysée palace now forms the rather incongruous setting of a boys' school run on military lines. The Kapurthala family has removed its residence to a building which seems to have come out of the 'Italian period' that followed on from Jagatjit Singh's 'French period'. The Villa Buona Vista is a shooting-lodge built by the Maharaja's state engineer, J. O. S. Elmore, in a formal garden on the forested banks of the river Beas. Thereafter there was a 'Spanish period' when the Maharaja married (and later divorced) a Spanish dancer. At the end of this long apprenticeship in European cultures it was hardly surprising that a senior Kapurthala prince should have converted to Christianity. He had to forgo the succession to the princely title which passed to his younger brother. Since Independence the Kapurthala ruler has taken a career in the Indian army and has been profusely decorated for his exploits in the 1972 war with Pakistan. But this reversion to the military roots of the Kapurthala family can in no way disguise the effect of the extraordinary monument to the culture of royal France which stares out across the wheatfields of the Punjab.

FARIDKOT

But for a characteristically Indian gesture of contrition Faridkot would have been named Mokal Har, after the thirteenth century Rajput warlord, Mokalsai. After carving out a territory in the western Punjab, Mokalsai set to work to build a fort. Amongst the labourers that his henchmen press-ganged into the work of construction was a renowned Muslim mystic, Sheikh Farid. As soon as Mokalsai discovered the mistake he took the holy man into his house, fell at his feet in apology and offered to make amends by naming the fortress in the holy man's honour. Sheikh Farid became the family's patron saint, Mokalsai's grandson embraced Islam, and Mokal Har became Faridkot.

The fortress changed hands in the Moghul period when Chaudhuri Kapura was appointed administrator of the area by the Moghul Emperor Akbar. Chaudhuri Kapura came from the same complex of families which founded the Patiala dynasty and many of the other Sikh states in the western Punjab. He served Akbar so faithfully that he even refused to harbour the tenth Sikh *guru*, Gobind Singh, when he was seeking refuge from Moghul soldiers. The *guru* cursed the house of Faridkot, and although he was later persuaded by the Chaudhuri's sons to with-

A drummer in Maharaja Harinder Singh's private band.

LEFT *Unusually tall palm trees grow in the garden of the Raj Mahal. Each year the palace is repainted in Eton blue.*

draw the curse, it seems to have had its effect. The *guru* predicted that the house of Faridkot would last no more than seven generations, and it was the seventh ruler in line from Chaudhuri Kapura who ceded the state to the Indian Union in 1948. The *guru* also predicted dynastic difficulties along the way and certainly the history of the Faridkot line during the transition from the eighteenth to the nineteenth centuries is among the bloodiest of the many bloody dynastic histories of the princely ruling houses.

This line of the family disappeared in the wars with Ranjit Singh at the turn of the century and another branch then moved to the centre of the stage. Here too the sons of the prince, Hamir Singh, started fighting over their inheritance even before their father was dead. When one eventually succeeded to the throne, *his* son immediately rebelled on the grounds that the father clearly preferred the son born to him by a Muslim concubine to his legitimate heir. The rebellion was successful and the ruler died in exile. At this point the new ruler's uncle returned to the battleground, fought and killed the rebellious son and took possession of the fort. He was then promptly murdered within a month.

This took the story to 1807 and there was now some respite because outside powers intervened. Ranjit Singh took over the state, which was not in much of a condition to offer resistance, and the British promptly wrested it back on the grounds that it was on their side of the Sutlej river. The British somehow found a remnant of the ruling family to occupy the throne again, and almost immediately the family returned to its bad old ways. Gulab Singh was assassinated in 1826, and succeeded by his minor son who died, mysteriously and almost certainly nefariously, a year later at the age of five. Gulab Singh's brother took over and promptly faced a rebellion from a third brother. But enough was enough. By this time the estate was depopulated, the land had been reduced to a virtual desert and the stench of blood was becoming overpowering. The British sent in troops to quell the revolt and to confirm Gulab Singh's brother as the rightful ruler. After this, things settled down.

Until the end of the wars and the blood-letting the population had prudently been confined within the fort. After 1837, they began to move out and form a town below the walls. Prosperity gradually returned as the population filtered back. The Raja regained some territory for the usual acts of loyal service during the Mutiny and Afghan wars, the roads were metalled, the railway arrived – an important railway junction was located within the state – and the Sirhind irrigation canal brought a promise of wealth. In the 1870s and 1880s Raja Bikram Singh employed retired British officials to revitalise his civil administration, and borrowed officers from the British Indian Army to reorganise his own troops. A bank set up business in Faridkot in 1875, new bazaars were built in 1885, and schools, hospitals and other public works sprang up regularly as

Faridkot rode a wave of prosperity into the twentieth century. It was time for Raja Bikram Singh also to come down from his old fort and build a palace.

Raj Mahal was built in the style of the colonial bungalow. This style evolved in the hands of engineers and amateur architects who, in the early days of the British Raj, had to build buildings habitable by Europeans throughout the interior of India. The style probably has a basis in the seaside architecture of Europe, particularly that of southern Europe with its strong Arabic influence. The style matured in the buildings that crowded the forts, 'factories' and settlements of Britain's early maritime empire, and thus the colonial style of India is closely related to a colonial style in other British territories. In the buildings in the Indian interior the chief aim of the designer was to defeat the sun. He used a variety of balconies, canopies, *verandahs* and screens to exclude the direct rays of the sun, and built with solid materials to improve insulation. The rooms were large with high ceilings, and were opened to the breeze through large arches on as many sides as possible. Such buildings were built with local materials, usually brick and wood, and with the help of local craftsmen, and thus they tended to borrow flourishes from the architecture of their particular location.

Raj Mahal follows this pattern. It was built by Mistri Jagat Singh who was heir to a tradition of building craftsmen. There are touches of the Rajput style in some of the gateways and friezes, and touches of the Punjabi town-house in the parapets and colonnades of the upper storey; but otherwise the strong arches and rippling balconies owe much to the tradition of the colonial bungalow, though there are significant differences. Few colonial bungalows rambled over an area of three acres, or were set in a park of twenty, And very, very few colonial bungalows were painted Eton blue.

Bikram Singh also took an interest in learning. He gave lavish patronage to the new Punjab University and was rewarded with an Honorary Fellowship. He also helped Sikh scholars and encouraged them to write treatises on the holy book of the Sikhs, the Guru Granth Sahib. Finally he constructed Sikh temples both within the state and at the Kashmiri capital of Srinagar. But even this could not avert Guru Gobind Singh's prediction. In 1948 Bikram Singh had to merge his state into the new country of India, but he took this little matter in his stride. He gave up ruling, took instead to agriculture and became one of the most progressive farmers of the Punjab. But he made no attempt to lower himself to the lifestyle of the humble farmer; he continued to occupy his palace, kept armed guards at the gate, and maintained a palace band to perform every weekend and on special occasions.

Weeding a lawn.

KASHMIR

Everybody wanted Kashmir. In succession the Moghuls, the Afghans and the British conquered it. As his last wish the Emperor Jahangir expressed a desire to possess it personally. Ranjit Singh annexed it. A Punjabi chieftain clambered into the ruling seat. The British called it 'an earthly paradise' and 'the loveliest spot on the face of the earth'. Jawaharlal Nehru thought it was 'like some supremely beautiful woman'. India and Pakistan have twice fought over it.

None of them can really be blamed for their cupidity. The princely state which emerged in the nineteenth century was originally a collection of different principalities. In the very south is the state of Jammu where the plains of the Punjab creep into the foothills of the Himalayas. From here the densely wooded hills rise through a series of gorges and steep mountain passes. On all sides are orchards growing pears, walnuts, guavas and the biggest apples in the world. In the distance are views of snow-capped peaks. Over the last pass the road descends into the great high valley of Kashmir. Here sits the capital, Srinagar, amid an expanse of lakes, floating gardens and lush forests. Half the population lives in the ramshackle wooden houses which line the rivers and backwaters, and the rest on islands and houseboats in the lake. The principal form of transport is not the car, not even the horse or donkey, but the *shikara* or canoe. Beyond, the hills start to climb more steeply, the lushness of the

The Baradari palace faces a row of houseboats across the river Jhelum. The austerely classical palace is now abandoned.

Srinagar valley gives way to the harsh, grey, craggy terrain of high mountains cut through with great, stern glaciers. In the corrugations of these mountains lies a series of remote and fantastic hill states with names which smack more of Tibet and central Asia than India – Gilgit, Hunza, Ladakh, Baltistan, Chilas, Rupshu and Zaskar. Here there is always snow, occasionally herds of goat with nomadic keepers, remote monasteries, lynxes and wild mink. Finally one hits the great wall of the Karakoram Himalayas, rising up to 28,250 feet on the peak of K2. Just beyond is a muddle of international frontiers – Nepal, Tibet, China, Russia, Pakistan and the incongruous long sliver of the Pamirs poking up from Afghanistan.

The state of Kashmir in (more or less) this form stretches back less than a century, but the history of the region goes back to the wanderings of Alexander the Great and beyond. It was only in the late eighteenth century that the history of the lowland state of Jammu and that of the highland valley of Kashmir began to collide, and only in the late nineteenth century that the mountain states were absorbed. But the backwash of so many imperial and local designs had already left an untidy litter of peoples.

The early part of the history belongs entirely to the vale of Kashmir. There was a succession of Buddhist and then Hindu kingdoms in the valley but these were consigned to the relative obscurity of archaeological remains by the arrival of the Muslim invaders in 1339. For the warriors from the deserts of Persia and central Asia the lush valley must have seemed like the heaven of gentle breezes, flowers and cool, rippling streams promised in the Holy Koran. The Moghul Emperors, and Jahangir in particular, set out to cure whatever imperfections the valley still had by planting strong Chenar trees, building fine palaces and fashioning the delicate, formal Moghul gardens which still remain. In the meantime they brought virtually all of the population but the stubborn Brahmins into the Muslim faith. As Moghul power receded the Afghans swept down and from 1752 to 1819 Kashmir was a province of Afghanistan.

Up to this point, the history of Jammu was bound up with the warlike history of the Punjab. The Dogra Rajputs had once ruled in the area but had been despatched by the Muslim invasion. When Moghul power retreated, the Dogras briefly regained their patrimony but after 1780 the ruler of Jammu, just like the other princes of the Punjab, was absorbed by the expansionist Sikh kingdom of Ranjit Singh. However, the Jammu Dogras served so loyally, and the hilly principality of Jammu was so difficult to control from the plains, that Ranjit Singh allowed Gulab Singh of Jammu to remain as a semi-independent Raja.

In 1819, Ranjit Singh conquered the valley of Kashmir and annexed it to his kingdom. In the wake of Ranjit's death, the British defeated the Sikhs and demanded a huge indemnity. The Sikhs could not pay so they offered to hand over Kashmir in lieu of the money. The British had not yet thought about the strategic importance of the north-east frontier and had little idea of the delights of Kashmir. They turned down the offer. Gulab Singh of Jammu entered the negotiations as a mediator, let it be known that he was quite prepared to take the tiresome problem of Kashmir's future off everybody's hands, and emerged from the treaty of 1846 virtually as the independent king of the combined states of Jammu and Kashmir. The British were later criticised for selling Kashmir for a handful of silver or, more accurately, for seventy-five lakhs of rupees and an annual tribute of six embroidered shawls and a dozen mountain goats.

Once the Sikhs were settled, the British began to think more seriously about the commercial and political importance of the north-eastern region. Russian expansion into central Asia made this frontier appear to men in Whitehall as one of the tenderest spots of the British Empire, and thus began the intrigue and excitement of the 'Great Game'. Meanwhile the routes that wandered up through the valley of Kashmir to the Himalayan passes beyond conveyed one of India's most ancient and valuable trades to all parts of northern Asia. With the encouragement of the British, and the help of the armies of Punjabi Sikhs and Jammu Dogras, Gulab Singh set out to integrate into his domain the handful of small principalities scattered through the high valleys of the mountain chain. These little regions were, under the control of the state of Kashmir, to act as 'the outworks of the British Empire in this quarter'.

This completed the demographic muddle. Gulab Singh, a Hindu prince with a largely Hindu soldiery and a British overlord, ruled over a population which consisted partly of Muslim peasants and partly of Buddhist and tribal people from the mountains, along with a smattering of Brahmin intellectuals, and some pockets of Sikh and Afghan settlers left over from recent periods of conquest.

It was not that the Raja was insecure, or that the people of the state were badly at loggerheads with one another. Gulab Singh and his successors settled down to a period of quietly successful rule. The winters were spent in the lowlands of Jammu. Here in the 1880s Gulab Singh's son built the Mondi Palace on the densely wooded hills overlooking the Tavi river. In the early twentieth century, Maharaja Sir Pratap Singh gave over this building to serve as the state's first High Court and built the more modern and spacious Amar Singh Mahal in a style which was partly copied from the builders of Imperial Delhi. In the summer, the rulers moved up to the other capital of Srinagar in the vale of Kashmir. Here Gulab Singh first lived in Sher Garhi, the sprawling fort in the centre of the city, but this was soon replaced by the Baradari palace on the banks of the Jhelum river. This enabled the Maharaja to make his annual progress to the summer capital into a remarkable pageant. He arrived at his palace by way of the river in a huge galley rowed by regally dressed oarsmen and followed by a flotilla

of other smaller craft. A wide flight of steps led up from the river to the palace whose interior, according to one British visitor:

The Mondi palace overlooking the Tavi river in Jammu now houses the High Court.

'is much glare and glitter, large mirrors and huge chandeliers of coloured glass, but the walls and ceilings are unique, being covered with papier mâché painted in beautiful devices'.

Beside the palace stood the family temple, for in this sea of Buddhism and Islam the Dogra rulers kept up a reputation for Hindu orthodoxy. European visitors at the Residency complained of being woken at three in the morning by the gunshot that aroused the Maharaja for prayer; the sacred cows on the streets were zealously protected by the state; and the Maharaja employed a customs service to ensure that the European guests did not import tins of Bovril or other unmentionable foods. Indeed the Maharajas of Kashmir, even though their territory was larger than that of any other Indian state, acquired a reputation for

The Hari Niwas, built in the early twentieth century, contains a renowned collection of miniatures of the Dogra school.

asceticism and restraint which was quite unusual amongst their peers. Even so the ceiling of the private temple in the Baradari palace was 'covered in thin plates of gold'.

As Kashmir became gradually more accessible (largely through the roads built for military purposes) so it became a favourite resort first of the officers of the Raj, then of the rich travellers of the whole world, and finally of the wealthy holiday-makers from the Indian plains. Maharaja Sir Hari Singh also made sure he enjoyed the glamour of his summer residence, and built an elegant palace in the style of a millionaire's country club set in immaculate gardens on a hill beside the famous Dal Lake. This was later to become a luxury hotel.

The people of Kashmir were rarely rich, but they were also rarely disgruntled and the advance of tourism at least brought some sort of prosperity. Although the passage of the seasons is no longer marked by the migration of the Maharaja from one palace to another, the valley of Kashmir still serves as the axis of a remarkable seasonal movement of people. In the hot months of the early summer, families from the scorched north Indian plain move up to the gentler climate of Kashmir and, as if by chain reaction, at the same time the nomadic tribesmen of the Himalayas drive their flocks of sheep and goats out of the valley and up to the high mountain pastures.

COOCH BEHAR

A copy of the dome of St Peter's, Rome dominates the façade of the palace at Cooch Behar. The gardens contain two tennis courts, a nine-hole golf course and a polo ground.

Cooch Behar is a geographical oddity. It sits where the ripples of the eastern Himalayas flow out of the little mountain kingdom of Bhutan and onto the flat watery plains of Bengal. It also straddles the neck of the valley through which the great Brahmaputra river flows down from Assam. Although it seems to be part of the hilly country of the north-eastern frontier of India, the state itself is a flat plain hardly more than three hundred feet above sea level. It is strewn with rivers, lakes and marshes; and when the great Brahmaputra or the temperamental Tista river, which drains down the melting snows of Kanchenjunga, are feeling unkind, the state is virtually submerged. It is surrounded by hilly kingdoms and states – Nepal, Sikkim, Bhutan and the tribal divisions of the Meghalaya hills. Even now the region of Cooch Behar nestles amid a tangle of international boundaries, and throughout its history it has served as a buffer state between the rich, deltaic civilisation of Bengal and the tribal peoples of the Himalayan foothills. More recently it has become famous for its tigers and its 'romances'.

The earliest of these buffer states was probably the Kamrup kingdom which lasted until the Muslims overran Bengal in the fifteenth century. But the Muslims did not settle the area, and the warring tribes and petty chiefs from the Bhutan hills flowed down onto the plains. One of these tribes was the Koch and by the sixteenth century they had mastered the area and thrown up a dynasty. The Koch (now known as Rajbansis) still form the majority of the population and provide the 'Cooch' in the state's title. Later the region served as a buffer between the Moghul rulers in Bengal and the Bhutanese and Assamese warlords in the hills. In 1773, the British East India Company made a treaty with the Cooch Behar ruler with the same aim of protecting the northern flank of the Company's expanding empire in Bengal. But the treaty did not preclude problems for the new allies. The Raja hired a certain Mr Tobias Wagner to intercede with the Company to improve the terms of the treaty, but Warren Hastings, the Governor-General, responded by having Mr Wagner unceremoniously deported as a 'European vagabond'. The Raja suffered so greatly from the inroads of the European carpet-bagging merchants in the years immediately following the treaty that in 1780 he signed away half of his territory to the Company in order to be rid of the trouble. The early nineteenth century saw a return to the dynastic feuds, and when a minority occurred in the ruling house in 1863 the British felt it was time to move in, reorganise the state's administration and cultivate an ideal prince.

This was the start of the history of tiger-shooting and romances. The marshy elephant grass of the Cooch Behar plain was a perfect refuge for the tiger, and Cooch Behar was conveniently close to the concentration of European officials in the old capital of Calcutta. Up to 1950 the Maharaja maintained countless elephants trained for tiger-hunts. The romances began with the minor prince, Nripendra Narain, whom the

The *interior of the dome mimics the Raphael-esque designs from the Roman original.*

Chippendale-style mirrors and console-tables, an elaborately painted and gilded ceiling and brocaded walls in the yellow drawing-room.

British set out to train as a model ruler. He passed through the hands of a number of British tutors, was sent to the school especially set up for the sons of Indian nobility in Benares, and finally went on to the premier institution of higher education in India at the time, Presidency College at Calcutta. He was then whisked off to Europe to complete this apprenticeship to power, but first it was necessary to conclude a marriage. His British mentors insisted that the bride should have an education to match the one that they had carefully bestowed on the future prince, but in mid-nineteenth century India this stipulation considerably narrowed down the field. Eventually they chose Sunity Devee, the daughter of a great Calcutta intellectual, Babu Keshub Chandra Sen. Her education had clearly been ideal; at the prospective couple's first meeting she did not sing or dance in the Indian manner but instead played a minuet on the piano.

But there were considerable difficulties in the way of the match. Keshub Chandra Sen was a leading member of the Brahmo Samaj, a religious reform society which wished to cleanse Hinduism of its excesses of ritualism, idolatry and superstition and to insert in their place elements of intellectual and social humanism which had clearly been borrowed from Christianity. It was the social progressivism of the Brahmos that had led Sen to educate his daughter so well and thus to catch the eye of the British matchmakers. But the orthodox members of the Cooch Behar family thought Brahmoism was certainly not Hinduism and probably almost Christianity, and consequently disliked the idea of such a marriage. Keshub Chandra Sen was keen on the match until he found that the British wanted to conclude the marriage quickly in order to take their ward off to Europe; for this haste would mean his daughter would have to be married below the age which, Sen himself had recently argued from the speakers' rostrums and council chambers of Calcutta, should be the legal age of consent. In a welter of backstairs intrigue which lasted until the eve of the ceremony, these problems were gradually ironed out.

This curious match between Sunity Devee from one of the most progressive families of febrile, urbane Calcutta and Nripendra Narain from the flooded semi-tribal backwater of princely India was a remarkable success. Even the British officials, who had played the role normally reserved for the village barber in such affairs, were remarkably pleased. Nripendra Narain became a Brahmo, and with the help of his active wife filled his state with the institutions dear to the Victorian imperialist. Indeed the main square of Cooch Behar emerged as a microcosmic model of Benthamite principles – two schools, a court-house, a jail, a state record room and a printing office.

The second romance involved their younger son, Jitendra Narain. At the resplendent balls associated with the Delhi Coronation Durbar of George V in 1911, Jitendra Narain danced with a daughter of the

French porcelain clock.

A cool verandah *with trophies of
hunting in Cooch Behar's famous game
reserves.*

Maharaja of Baroda. The romance that followed was far from straight-
forward. The Cooch Behar family was now firmly Brahmoist by faith,
and the Baroda family could not brook a match with such people.
Through a trail of scorned engagements, secret trysts, smuggled notes
and family rows the story of the romance crept slowly into the gossip
columns of the Indian and then of the British press. It continued with
a cat-and-mouse chase through the *salons*, pullman cars and ballrooms
of Europe with Jitendra and the Princess Indira trying to get together
and the Baroda family and its entourage desperately trying to keep them
apart. It ended with a marriage at Harrow Road Registry Office in 1913.
Three weeks later Jitendra's elder brother died and Jitendra and
Indira became the Maharaja and Maharani of Cooch Behar. The Baroda
family fumed for five years but finally, on the racecourse at Poona, were
reconciled to their daughter and her new family.

*A scion of the Cooch Behar royal house
was presented with a set of gilt and
tapestry chairs by his godmother,
Queen Victoria.*

The third romance concerned Gayatri Devi, a daughter of the Maharaja of Cooch Behar. While the Brahmoist Sunity Devee had forced monogamy and modernism onto the remote state, Gayatri Devi, who grew up in the dedicatedly modern atmosphere of Cooch Behar, seemed to put the process into reverse. She insisted in going off and agreeing to become a third wife in the prestigious, but nevertheless traditionalist, house of Jaipur. She, of course, quite swept the Maharaja of Jaipur off his feet, thrust her rival wives firmly into the shade, and went on to make her mark in both princely society and national politics.

The new palace built by Sunity Devee and her husband expressed their concern for progress and learning. It was, as Sunity Devee recorded, 'designed by a Western architect and built in an eclectic style' but in fact the dome and the Durbar hall beneath it are remarkably good examples of Renaissance Italian style. The model for both the interior and exterior of the dome was clearly St Peter's at Rome, and in copying the Raphael-esque decoration for the inside of the Cooch Behar Durbar hall the architect was only following a fashion which dominated Europe at the time. The rest of the palace, however, was rather more cavalier in its choice of styles. The pediments at either end of the exterior (later removed after earthquake damage) were severely Roman, and the whole was supposed to resemble a comfortable Etruscan villa. Yet the dominating use of the red brick of eastern India gives it a strange resemblance (with the addition of some regal flourishes) to the style that marked many of the schools and colleges built by the Raj. Inside were the emblems of the hunt – the tusks of the Maharaja's favourite elephants at the foot of the staircase, the mementoes of the chase in the colonnaded passageways – and the soft colours of genteel romance: one drawing room walled in yellow brocade, and another with a pink carpet, woven specially in Iran. Finally, as Sunity Devee enthused, 'On one side of the palace is the swimming bath, and covered racket and tennis courts. The gardens are lovely.'

Beyond this cool inner courtyard lie three kitchens – one Bengali, one Mahrathi and one European.

TRIPURA

The north-eastern frontier of the Indian subcontinent is one of the most complicated areas in the world. To the north live the Mongoloid peoples of the great Himalayan wall, and the territories of Tibet and China lie beyond. To the east lie the serried ranks of the rivers that have created the alluvial plain of Indo-China with their local populations of Mons, Thais, Laos, Viets and Khmers. To the west lie the great river deltas of the Ganges and Brahmaputra and the ancient civilisation of the north Indian plain. Just to complete the confusion of the region, the Himalayas throw out a five-hundred-mile spur of hills which stretches down to the Bay of Bengal. This spur provides the natural frontier between the Indian subcontinent and the Burmese state stretched along the Irrawaddy river. As the civilisations of China, India, and Indo-China expanded towards their natural limits, this spur of hills became the refuge of tribes and peoples who fled from the advance of civilisation and overrule. Mizos, Chins, Kachins, Nagas, Lushais and a host of smaller tribes collect in the nooks and crannies of these remote hills. The settled civilisations of the plains have generally been content to leave these independent and warlike people alone, to let them act as unbiassed hostile guards of this natural frontier, and only to enter and disrupt the region in times of political ambition or political insecurity. Thus the population of this tract includes a huge mixture of racial types, a cacophony of local languages, a bizarre mingling of social traits borrowed from the neighbouring civilisations, and an overlying backwardness, remoteness and distrust of the outside world.

The twentieth century has demanded that all the territory of the earth should be mapped, attributed and accounted for. Not surprisingly, this demand has turned an area such as India's north-eastern frontier into a tangle of international boundaries and a clutch of insoluble political problems. It is this which has turned Tripura into one of the great geographical mistakes of modern history. When the British left the subcontinent in 1947 and the princes were invited to accede to one of the resulting nation states of India and Pakistan, it was not surprising that the Hindu ruler and the people of Tripura should choose to cleave to India, But this made Tripura a wedge of territory which jutted into the edge of eastern Pakistan and almost cut off the bulk of that country from its second major port of Chittagong. At the same time, Tripura was almost entirely cut off from its own mother country of India. There was not a single road connecting Tripura to any part of India and until one was built, with great speed, the aeroplane provided the only contact between the two. Then in 1971 East Pakistan prised itself away from West Pakistan and constituted the new state of Bangladesh. The fighting which accompanied the division of the subcontinent in 1947 and the redivision in 1971 precipitated two huge waves of refugees into the anomalous little backwater of Tripura. There was no way to stop this flight from misery even though it swamped the local people

*The Ujjayanta Palace is approached
up a massive European-style staircase.*

*The people of Agartala come daily to
the two large water tanks in front of
the palace to bathe and do their washing.*

of Tripura, buried the local population of half a million under the weight of more than a million immigrants, devastated the forests, pushed the wildlife further into the hills and turned the delightful capital, Agartala, into a sprawling shanty town.

The origins of this sad little modern anomaly lie in the area's history. The region was always geographically disposed to act as a buffer-state; while the extraordinary history of Tripura's last millennium ensured that it was a *Hindu* buffer-state amid a *tribal* population, and then surrounded that Hindu state with a *Muslim* population and leaders.

The British called it 'Hill Tipperah' but that name evokes a completely false image associated with the cool climate, rugged Himalayan back-drop and imported comforts of the British hill station. In fact, Tripura was only a region of warm, gently ambling hills clinging to the inside edge of the frontier chain. It had a small and scattered population, mostly living at the foot of the hills on the very edge of the plain of Bengal, and a remote, sleepy, well-wooded township for its capital at Agartala. The ruling family originated from a series of vagrant warrior chiefs who could trace their wanderings over several centuries from the north Indian plain, through the valley of Assam, to the hills of the north-eastern frontier. This trek was a microcosm of the process that, over a much greater span of years, had populated these hills with a morass of tribal fragments. The ruling clan had arrived in Tripura by the four-teenth century, carved a kingdom out of the tribal population by pretty lavish use of the sword, and immediately claimed that their dynasty already stretched back over ninety-nine generations. They had probably also brought with them literate culture and the Hindu religion. Indeed the Rajmala, or Chain of Kings, which makes the claim of dynastic longevity, is reckoned to be the oldest extant composition in the Bengali language, and it may well owe both its composition and its survival to the fact that none of the new Tripura Raja's subjects could read it. Certainly, too, the turn of the sixteenth century saw the construc-tion of Hindu temples in the region; and their distinctive design – which could be described as the rounded dome of a Buddhist stupa placed over the ramshackle simplicity of a tribal hut – sums up the mixture of cultures which were now subsumed within the new religion.

The Moghuls arrived in Bengal at the turn of the seventeenth century and their viceroy, the Nawab of Murshidabad, defeated the Raja of Tripura and sacked his capital without much difficulty in 1618. But the Nawab's forces were very quickly driven back to the plains, not by the military force of the Tripura Raja, but by an epidemic of some outlandish submontane disease. Moreover, the Moghul Nawab soon realised that Tripura could act as a perfect buffer-state and that it was not necessary to stay in this little hilly kingdom and exercise direct control. The Burmese Sultan of Arakan was wont to march up through these hills on periodical expeditions of aggrandisement and loot, while the Lushai and Kuki tribes in the higher hills beyond Tripura were known for their intemperateness and their dislike of the lowlander. Thus the Raja was left with his little Hindu kingdom, while under the weight of Moghul rule the vast majority of the Bengali population was welcomed into the fold of Islam. Herein lay the knotty political problems of 1947 and 1971. The Hindu kingdom of Tripura had become surrounded by tribal hill people on one flank, and Muslim peasants and grandees on the other.

By the time the British began to replace Moghul power in Bengal in the mid-eighteenth century, Tripura was well-established as a political anomaly and a convenient buffer-state. Naturally enough, the British found in the Raja of Tripura an early ally against their common enemy, the Moghul Nawabs. The British marched into Tripura in 1761 on the excuse of settling a dispute between the Raja and some Bengali neighbours, but just like their Moghul predecessors the British were not anxious to occupy the region, and thus made a treaty with the Tripura ruler and retired. Throughout the period of British rule in India Tripura remained remote and independent. It was rarely visited by officialdom. The British merely froze the political situation and left it to be disentangled amid the welter of religious jealousies which they finally left behind in 1947.

The palace of the Tripura rulers is a monument to the cultural bewilderment of a dynasty which clung to the Hindu religion, ruled over a largely tribal population, was almost surrounded by a Muslim territory, and was guaranteed by a Christian government. The Raja responded to the comparatively settled conditions of the nineteenth century with attempts to take a firmer grip on his subjects. First he tried to impel them towards a more convincing attachment to the Hindu religion, but this provoked riots and ended in a miserable failure. Turning away from this strategy, the Raja decided to bestow on his subjects as many of the blessings of the west as he could afford. He codified the laws, abolished slavery, constructed roads, and built a school, a museum, a jail and a Victoria Memorial Hospital. It was in this mood that at the turn of the century the old town was badly damaged by an earthquake and the Maharaja Radhakishore set out to build a palace 'more dignified and suitable than his predecessors have been able to provide'. He hired one British and one Indian architect, Sir Alexander Martin and Sir R. N. Mukherji, and let them loose on a seventy-acre park and a budget of ten *lakhs* of rupees. They turned the park into a huge landscaped garden in an imitation of Moghul style, with geometric flower-beds, artificial lakes and patterns of fountains, and placed in the middle of it a vast building in an attempted synthesis of Moghul and Italian Renaissance styles. On the sky-line Moghul kiosks and canopies vie with classical domes. Below, Moghul arches intervene in Italianate colonnades and heavy European staircases lead up to mock-Persian porticoes. This crumbling, white Ujjayanta Palace seems to have been designed more as a dignified monument than a place of habitation. The interior is packed with reception rooms, Durbar halls, banqueting halls and other public spaces so that there is no room for living quarters. The princely family lived in adjoining annexes. The palace served mainly as a private museum, a repository for their magnificent collection of paintings, *objets d'art* and rare oriental manuscripts.

Perhaps because of this, Radhakishore's successor built some rather more comfortable alternative residences. The summer palace is a low, cool building set beside a lake, accessible only by boat, and replete with memories of Moghul design. The Kunjaban was built on a hillock to the north of the capital and surrounded with orchards and a small zoo. Its open *verandah* with a view out over the Baramura hills became a favourite retreat of the great Bengali poet, Rabindranath Tagore. The

In 1932 Maharaja Bir Bikram Kishore built the Neer Mahal in the middle of Lake Sonamura for his wife who was homesick for her native place of Udaipur. The palace was furnished in traditional style with two hundred carpets and little other furniture.

Neer Mahal was abandoned in 1944 when the level of the lake dropped. In the distance the ghostly palace seems enormous but is in fact no more than a chain of narrow buildings linked by walkways.

Tripura family claimed to be among the first to recognise the genius of Tagore, and Tagore repaid the compliment by using the career of a seventeenth-century Tripura prince as the central character of one of his novels. But that was when Tripura was still a sleepy backwater of colonial India, and before it became the refuge of the displaced persons of post-colonial wars.

RAMPUR

Until the fifteenth century the region to the east of Delhi was covered with subtropical jungle and inhabited by robbers who preyed on the capital city and the trade routes leading down into the Ganges valley. The Great Moghuls determined to clear the area and, to kill two birds with one stone, they parcelled out much of the land to the Afghan freebooters and mercenaries as a reward for service in the Moghul armies; this was an astute move since the Afghans had already seized most of the territory without asking. As Moghul power weakened at the turn of the eighteenth century, one of the Afghan warriors, Sayyad Ali Muhammad, who originally came from Kandahar, emerged as a powerful local chieftain. By 1719 he had carved out his own state and forced the Moghuls to grant recognition. The men of the Indian plains called these Afghans Rohillas, which roughly meant 'men of the mountains', and the area which they made their own was known as Rohilkand.

The emergent state continued to expand up to 1750, and by this time the Moghul Emperor had been forced to grant the new dynasty the title of Nawab. But this rapid rise to power and prestige annoyed and disquieted the more established Nawab in the neighbouring state of Oudh, and also aroused the jealousies of both the British and Maratha forces who were prospecting for empire at this time. The Nawab of Oudh eventually arranged an unholy alliance with the British East India Company and subcontracted to them the duty of crushing the upstart Rohilla state for a fee of five million rupees. The contract was fulfilled, the Rohillas scattered, and the Company paid. This particular transaction was later to figure prominently in the impeachment of the Governor-General of the time, Warren Hastings.

All but one of the Rohilla chiefs were killed or forced to surrender their estates. Only Sayyad Faizulla Khan escaped to the mountains and later returned to make his peace with his old neighbours. He

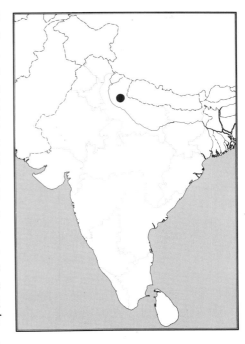

A life-size bronze horse and other ornaments stand in the grounds of the enormous Khas Bagh palace.

224

became a tributary to the state of Oudh until 1801 when the British forced the Nawab of Oudh to surrender Rohilkand to the Company. By this time Rampur had become the last refuge of Rohilla power and all the remnants of the expansionist phase now collected together in Rampur's new and expanding capital. Sayyad Faizullah Khan built an enormous bamboo hedge around the perimeter of this little island of Afghan power.

In 1857 the ruler kept Rohilkand quiet while the mutinous troops swirled past the state's borders. He gave protection to several British refugees, and even kept up the postal service into the disturbed area. As the British later noted, this was 'particularly singular among a strictly Mohammedan population bristling with arms, prone to plunder, greedy of gain and intolerant of Europeans'. The Nawab was rewarded with territory and titles, and his continued loyalty over the rest of the century (the time of the Afghan wars) equipped the Rampur Nawab with a string of titles which by 1909 nicely bracketed the flow of Persian glorification between parentheses of European origin: Colonel His Highness Alijah, Farzand-i-Dilpazir, Daulat-i-Inglisha, Mukhlis-ud-Daula, Nasir-ul-Mulk, Amir-ul-Umara, Nawab Sir Mohammed Hamid Ali Khan Bahadur, Mustaid Jang, G.C.I.E.

However the British rulers had little need to flatter the Rohilkand prince so heavily, for it seems he had by this time renounced war in favour of culture. As Rohilla power had shrunk in the late eighteenth century Rampur had emerged not only as a bastion of Afghan arms but also as the resort of Afghan men of letters. Yusuf Ali Khan, who had kept Rohilkand quiet in 1857, was also a scholar in both Arabic and Persian and a patron of the arts. Hamid Ali Khan, who came to the throne in 1896, could recite Urdu and Persian poetry by the hour and improvise couplets in several languages. His successor, Sayyad Raza Ali, was a versatile musician, a composer of great distinction, and a patron of Indian classical music, who attracted musicians from all over India to the Rampur court. He made a collection of musical instruments, many of them very old and all of them richly decorated. He also completed a work begun by his predecessors and brought together a collection of fifteen thousand oriental manuscripts, which included a volume of Persian verse with annotations written in the margins by the Emperors Babur and Shah Jahan. These were housed in a library along with an outstanding collection of miniature paintings dating from the sixteenth to eighteenth centuries and including portraits of Babur and of the great seventeenth-century traveller, François Bernier. After Independence, the Raza library was given to the nation and now attracts research scholars from all over the world.

Hamid Ali Khan, the Nawab at the turn of this century, was far more than just a scholar. He was also a *raconteur*, *bon-vivant* and an administrator of great skill. He provided the foundations upon which

ABOVE AND RIGHT *Part of Sayyad Raza Ali's collection of musical instruments.*

he and his successors could build up the reputation of Rampur as a seat of learning. He laid a network of irrigation canals, set up cotton mills and a sugar refinery, and encouraged traditional local handicrafts such as perfumery, sword-making, ornamental pottery and lacquer-ware. He also initiated a phase of frantic building in the state capital with the addition of new court-houses, guest-houses, bazaars, schools, hospitals and artillery lines. In 1911 the Rampur Gazetteer exclaimed:

'Indeed the town has undergone so many changes not only in its external aspect but also in the mode of life of its inhabitants that it would be almost impossible even for a local man to find any resemblance between the Rampur of olden times and the Rampur of today.'

Hamid Ali Khan's ally in this enormous project of town planning was Mr W. C. Wright, who was made chief engineer and 'to whom the public works department of the state owes its origin'.

Mr Wright remodelled and retouched the old buildings within the fort and palace complex – the Rang Mahal, the Machchi Bhawan, the Imambara and the old Benazir and Badri-Muni palaces – and equipped the major buildings with electric light and electric fans. He then began to raise up, on the foundations of an old part of the fort, the enormous new palace, the Khas Bagh. The original idea for the palace simply grew and grew and it took twenty-five years to bring the project to its conclusion. The building displays a whole catalogue of architectural styles which in turn reflect a whole catalogue of roles which the ruler was bound to play. First of all he was a Muslim and the leader of a prominent family, and this required a large *zenana*, sealed off from the rest of the palace, and guarded by eunuchs with naked swords. Next he was a collector and patron of the arts, and for this he needed a wing equipped with a music room, an art gallery to house the Moghul miniatures, and a library to store the rare manuscripts. Next, he was a

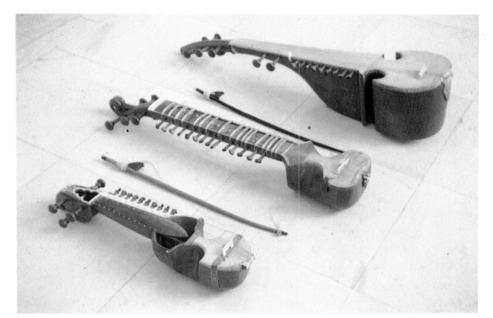

An early gramophone cabinet with the Islamic crescent moon and star on the top.

prince of British India, and thus he needed hospitable quarters to house his European guests. Rampur did not have the size and prestige to merit a visit from royalty, but it was obliged to receive a stream of British officials and these were accommodated within yet another section of the Khas Bagh. Finally there was the *mardaana*, the male counterpart to the *zenana*, which contained the Nawab's private apartments.

In 1923, the guest rooms of Khas Bagh accommodated the Viceroy, Lord Reading, and his wife in the course of their tour of north India. Lady Reading enjoyed her visit, partly because the Nawab presented her with a dress of 'gold tissue shot with mauve and all embroidered in bullion', partly because she was charmed by the Nawab's wife who had to lift up her colossal nose-ring every time she wished to eat and who explained that she could not go to Europe because there would be no fresh *pan* for her to chew, and partly because the state banquet was rounded off by a showing of the film of *Kismet*. Yet Lady Reading still endeavoured to find Rampur quaint and amusing; after all the Nawab was descended from a freebooting Afghan and thus he must have a streak of medieval ferocity. As she wrote to a friend:

'I forget if I told you he, the Nawab, put in a lift for me. When we arrived, lift did not work and we had to stand around for a quarter of an hour while man was found who had turned off the current. I would not be in that man's shoes but I don't suppose he has shoes now, they belong to his widow!'

Thus the wife of the guardian of Britain's eastern empire found it necessary to portray one of the most cultured rulers of northern India in the garb of the Queen of Hearts.

BENARES

Benares is the holiest city of the Hindus. Along the banks of the puri-fying Ganges river rise forts, mansions and temples, crowned by the aggressive outline of the mosque which Aurangzeb built as a calculated insult to his Hindu subjects. Pilgrimage to Benares, or Kashi as it is more commonly known, affords particular merit. People come from all over India to bathe from the stepped banks, or *ghats*, which line the northern waterfront. Many come to settle in retirement and die in Benares, for this increases the chance of favour in future lives. And traditionally every prospective bridegroom sets out to trek to Kashi and give himself up to a life of contemplation, but not too far from his own door is entreated by his relatives and persuaded to surrender himself instead to the life of the family.

Benares is full of sacred cows with no owners; men and women with no earthly cares; holy men with almost no clothes; and for well over a century it had a ruler with no kingdom.

The line of the Benares Rajas was founded in the early eighteenth century by a wealthy Brahmin, Mansa Ram. He secured a grant of the city and environs of Benares from the Nawab of Oudh, the Moghul governor of the region who, like all the Moghul governors in this period, was rapidly becoming an independent ruler. It was Mansa Ram's son, Balwant Singh, however, who firmly established the family. At the time, Benares was one of the largest and richest cities of northern India with an enormous income from the passage of pilgrims and from the commerce which flowed down the holy river. Balwant Singh set out to use that income in the style of an ideal Hindu prince. He first raised an army and built fortifications so that he might protect his subjects from the raids of Maratha armies, but then he turned his atten-tion to the religion and culture which were the lifeblood of the city. He helped to restore many of the temples which had suffered from neglect during Muslim overrule, patronised Hindu scholarship and fine arts, and wrote his own book of poetry.

In the reign of his successor, however, the troubles of the Benares line began. In 1776, the Nawab of Oudh was forced to cede the Benares domain to the British East India Company. The new Raja, Chait Singh, concluded a treaty with his new British overlords and for a time got on well with them. The Company entrusted Chait Singh with the manage-ment of their mint, and Chait Singh boasted that he offered his subjects a level of peace and prosperity which was without rival in the chaotic conditions of late eighteenth-century India:

'My fields are cultivated, my country is a garden, and my subjects are happy. My capital is the resort of the principal merchants of India and their treasures are deposited here.'

Indeed, Chait Singh's trouble was that he was far too successful. He had wealth at a time when the incessant fighting over the future of

The seventeenth-century ramparts of the Ramnagar palace rise up from the holy river Ganges.

northern India had driven most of the combatants towards bankruptcy. In his time as Governor-General of the East India Company, Warren Hastings lit upon the idea of squeezing money out of Chait Singh in order to save the Company's Indian operation from bankruptcy. He deliberately planned to make such extravagant demands on Chait Singh that he would eventually be obliged to protest; this protest would enable the Company, as Lord Macaulay later pointed out, 'to call his remonstrance a crime and punish him by confiscating all his possessions'.

Only in one essential did this plan miscarry. Chait Singh paid up the first few 'contributions' to Mr Hastings' coffers, added a straight bribe of £20,000, and then voiced the inevitable protest. The Company attacked, Chait Singh was put to flight, the palace was sacked and the estate confiscated. But Hastings never found the Raja's money. He believed that more than a million pounds' worth of treasure was hidden in the fort, but even after he had searched all the maidservants and

Princely India at its most sumptuous in the Durbar Hall of Ramnagar: a throne of sandalwood, gold and silk brocade and tiger-skins reclining on an enormous carpet presented by Lord Curzon, portraits of nine rulers staring down from the walls, and light filtering through delicate stained glass.

Detail of one of the long mirrors in the Durbar Hall.

230

ABOVE RIGHT *Five crystal chandeliers lit the Durbar Hall at night.*

A Durbar held during the spring festival of holi. *Against a background of dancing girls the Maharaja receives his subjects who file past and lay gifts of rupees at his feet.*

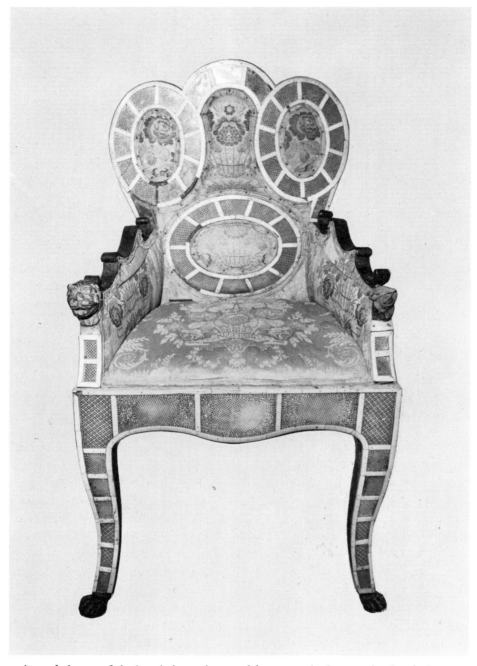

An ivory inlaid chair in the palace museum.

stripped them of their trinkets, he could not push the total seized above a quarter of that sum, and most of this disappeared as 'prize money' into the pockets of the soldiers who had conducted the assault.

The setting for these events was Ramnagar, the palace which Balwant Singh had built a mile above the city and on the opposite bank. From the river, according to Prevost Battersby who covered the Prince of Wales' visit in 1905, this 'curious fort-like Palace lies in flood-time like an ivory crown in the green swirl of the river, but now stands like a pleasure house above a donjon whose mighty stone bastions reach down to thrust their feet into the shrunken stream'. From the landward side it presented a view of grim, scarred battlements. Beyond these battlements were the inevitable stables and elephant sheds, then a series of courtyards, and finally the white tower of the palace perched on the bank of the river. The Maharaja's private apartments lay on one side of this tower, and the Durbar hall and reception rooms lay on the other.

232

The contrast between the two was enormous. The private rooms showed the imprint of an orthodox Hindu prince who resided by India's holiest river, bathed in it every day and took his responsibilities as a patron of Hindu culture very seriously indeed. Indeed the political eclipse which the Rajas of Benares suffered in the nineteenth century seems to have left them free to conduct their lives without too much attention to the swirling political and cultural currents of British India. Iswari Prasad Narain Singh, whose reign lasted for much of the mid-nineteenth century, loved music and poetry, invited all the famous performers of the day to his palace, and built up a fine collection of contemporary painting. The private apartments in which he and his successors lived in Ramnagar were not cluttered up with the accoutrements of a western life-style. There was almost no furniture, no unnecessary decoration, no concession to the world of progress and modernity.

The reception rooms, however, present an entirely different image, and these can still be seen since they have now been transformed into a museum. Even though the Raja of Benares had no kingdom, he was still credited with considerable status among Indian ruling families and was privileged to receive visits from members of the British royal family and other distinguished persons on tour. This gave the ruler the opportunity to turn his public reception rooms into a show-case for the arts and crafts in which the artisans of Benares excelled – wood and ivory inlaid work, and the famous 'Kincob' silk and gold brocade. The chairs, chests, and ceremonial coach doors of the Ramnagar palace are covered with intricate patterns of ivory inlaid into precious woods, while the Maharaja's barge sports a dramatic inlay in the pattern of a prancing horse. The rich tones of Kincob are used for the upholstery, curtains and wall-coverings, and in the Durbar hall this array of patterns and colours is set off by the rainbow of light admitted through the stained-glass doors and windows which climb up to the ceiling. Here the main

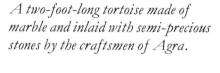

A two-foot-long tortoise made of marble and inlaid with semi-precious stones by the craftsmen of Agra.

LEFT *Ramnagar's river frontage in the evening light. The Maharaja's state barge can be seen in the background.*

ABOVE *The main courtyard leads off to the Durbar Hall on the left and the private apartments on the right.*

Elephants made of white marble and painted in their ceremonial regalia guard the entrance to the royal apartments.

An ivory and silver inlaid coach used on state occasions.

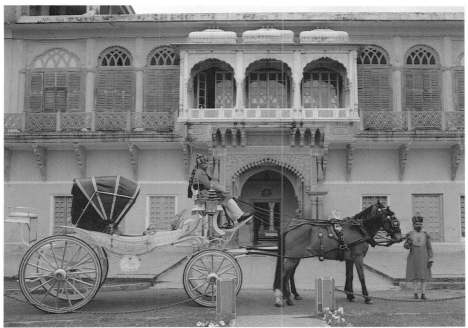

carpet is a gift from the most formidable of British Viceroys, Lord Curzon, and the smaller carpet before the Maharaja's throne is a gift from the Shah of Iran. The Durbar hall opens onto a wide terrace overlooking the Ganges. Here the distinguished visitors took tea and were treated to a display of fireworks.

Chait Singh had escaped by river and taken refuge in Gwalior. After the public outcry against Hastings' conduct, the Company restored part of the territory to Chait Singh's nephew, but the grant was in the form of landed estate, not a princedom, and there was no title. Moreover the city of Benares was reserved by the Company. For most of the century the Raja of Benares was not really a Raja and he did not rule Benares. Over the century, however, the residents of Ramnagar ingratiated themselves with their British overlords. When a house tax was imposed on Benares the people rose in revolt, closed the bazaars and 'inflammatory papers of the most objectionable tendency appeared placarded about the streets'. In the end, the British authorities called on the Raja to help resore order. Gradually, the family's privileges were returned and finally in 1911 the Viceroy restored the title of Maharaja and the power and privileges of a native prince. But the British still hung on to the rich city of Benares and the Maharaja never regained the city remarked in his own title.

The Maharaja would watch the sunset from a marble balcony overlooking the Ganges.

RIGHT *Two silver* howdahs *on show in the palace museum. One has sphinx handles, the other leopard handles.*

236

Liveried servants stand beneath the elephant gateway.

Sheltered by an ornate umbrella and followed by his personal entourage, the Maharaja sets off to watch his subjects celebrate the spring festival of holi.

239

EPILOGUE

The last of India's princely rulers *played* with great gusto. Sawai Man Singh made Jaipur the polo capital of India; among others excelling at this distinctively royal game were Hari Singh of Kashmir and Jagadendra Singh of Cooch Behar. Baroda, Patiala and Porbandar were names closely associated with the world of cricket; the Maharaja of Kashmir also played – although in his games the Maharaja's side always won and its princely captain always scored a half-century. Karni Singh of Bikaner shot clay-pigeons, Kolhapur was famous for pig-sticking, and there was hardly a princely ruler who had not shot his fair share of duck and tigers or had not cut a conspicuous (and usually rather portly) figure on the racecourses of India or England.

In 1949 they all ceased to be rulers but few of them ceased to be prominent. There were many, including Kolhapur, Kapurthala and Faridkot, who pursued distinguished careers in the army. There were others like Mysore, Kapurthala, Baroda and Porbandar who found a creative streak and produced books, musical compositions, poetry, paintings and works of philosophy. There were others like Kolhapur and Dungarpur who exchanged guns for binoculars and began to protect wildlife rather than shoot at it. And some also settled down to till the soil they had once ruled. Faridkot and Kutch have both made a name as centres of progressive farming.

For many of the princes, when they merged their states into the territory of independent India in 1949, merely broadened the stage on which they could play a ruling part. Karan Singh moved from the Maharaja's throne to the office of chief minister in Kashmir and then went on to serve, most appropriately for one who ruled over India's premier attraction, as minister for tourism in the central government. Krishnaraja Wadiyar of Mysore became the Governor in his own state and later of Madras. Karni Singh of Bikaner, Lakshman Singh of Dungarpur, the ex-ruler of Panna, and Madhav Rao Scindia of Gwalior, together with his mother, all won elections and sat in parliament. Fatesinghrao of Baroda moved on from the backbenches of parliament to serve as a minister at both state and national level. Sawai Man Singh of Jaipur served as Governor of Rajasthan, then as a parliamentarian and later as India's ambassador to Spain, while his Maharani continued after his death to hold a seat in parliament. Yadavindra Singh of Patiala went as India's representative to the United Nations, and then as ambassador to Rome and The Hague, while the ex-ruler of Kutch served as ambassador in Norway and as Deputy High Commissioner in London.

Neither the negligence of the departing British who shrugged off the responsibility of paramountcy, nor the diplomacy of Sardar Patel who persuaded the princes to cleave to India in 1949, nor the animosity of Mrs Gandhi who abolished the princes' pensions and privileges in 1970-71, could ever consign princely India to oblivion.

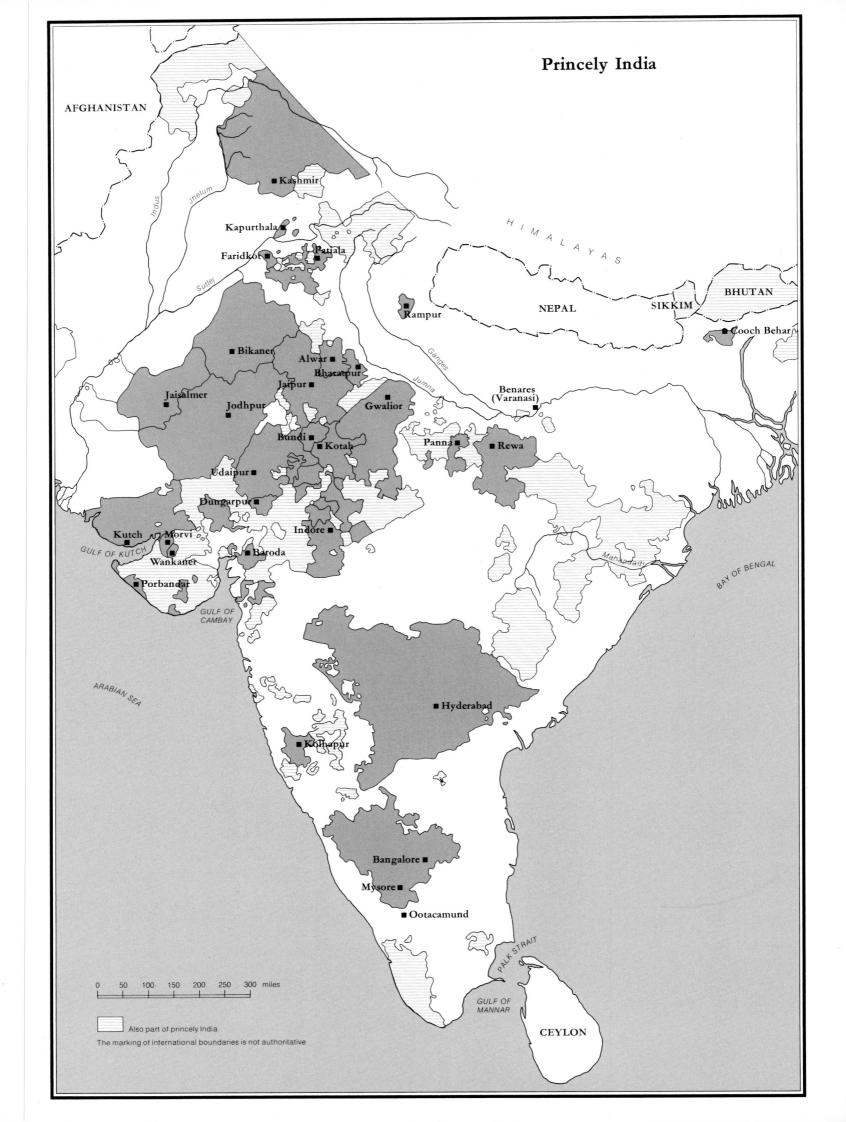

Princely India

AFGHANISTAN

Indus

Jhelum

■ Kashmir

Kapurthala ■

Sutlej

Faridkot ■   ■ Patiala

H I M A L A Y A S

■ Rampur

NEPAL

SIKKIM

BHUTAN

■ Cooch Behar

■ Bikaner

Alwar ■
Bharatpur

Ganges

■ Jaipur

Jumna

Benares
(Varanasi)
■

■ Jaisalmer

Jodhpur ■

■ Gwalior

Bundi ■
■ Kotah

Panna ■   ■ Rewa

Udaipur ■

Dungarpur ■

Indore ■

Kutch ■   Morvi ■

GULF OF KUTCH

Wankaner ■   ■ Baroda

Mahanadi

Porbandar ■

*GULF OF
CAMBAY*

BAY OF BENGAL

ARABIAN SEA

■ Hyderabad

■ Kolhapur

■ Bangalore

Mysore ■

■ Ootacamund

PALK STRAIT

0   50   100   150   200   250   300   miles

*GULF OF
MANNAR*

CEYLON

Also part of princely India

The marking of international boundaries is not authoritative

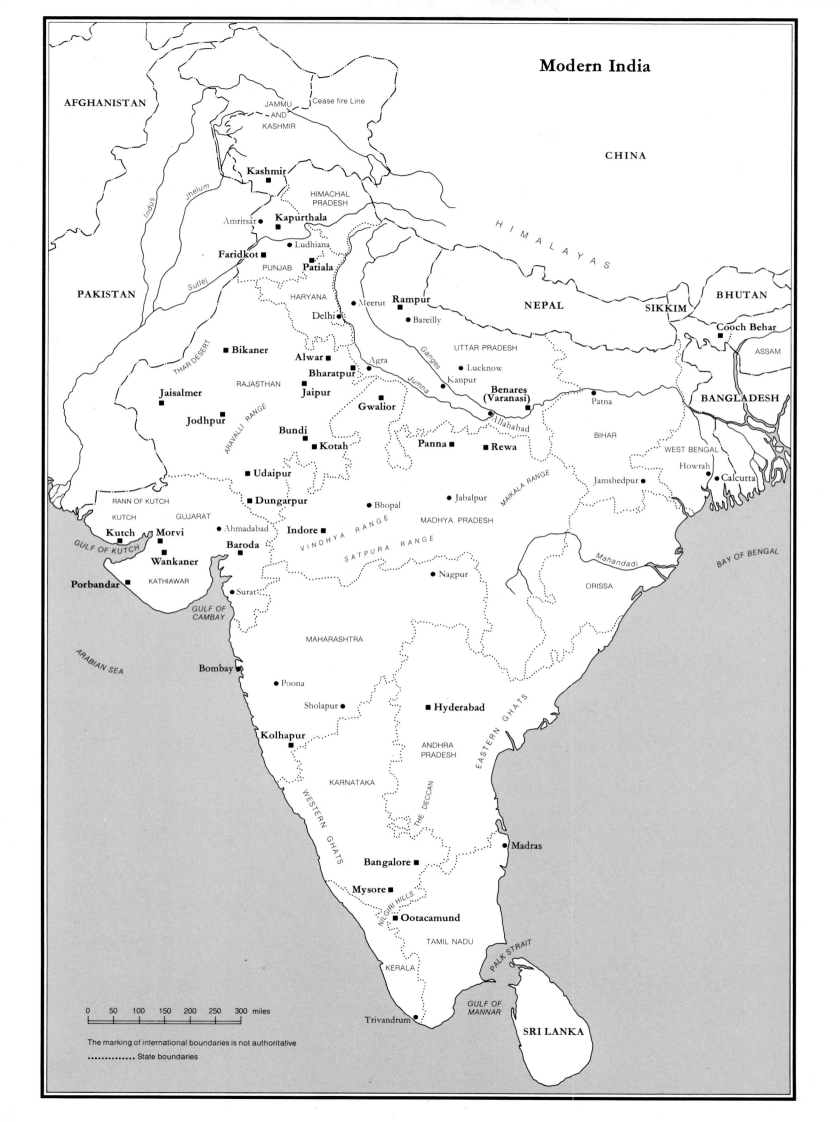

Modern India

AFGHANISTAN

JAMMU
AND
KASHMIR

Cease fire Line

CHINA

Indus

Jhelum

■ **Kashmir**

HIMACHAL
PRADESH

H I M A L A Y A S

Amritsar ● ■ **Kapurthala**

● Ludhiana

Faridkot ■

PUNJAB

Patiala ■

Sutlej

PAKISTAN

HARYANA

● Meerut **Rampur** ■

Delhi ■

● Bareilly

NEPAL

SIKKIM

BHUTAN

■ **Cooch Behar**

ASSAM

■ **Bikaner**

Alwar ■

Agra ●

● Lucknow

UTTAR PRADESH

Ganges

Bharatpur ■

Jumna

Kanpur ●

BANGLADESH

THAR DESERT

RAJASTHAN

Jaipur ■

**Benares
(Varanasi)** ■

Patna ●

Jaisalmer ■

Gwalior ■

Allahabad ●

ARAVALLI RANGE

Jodhpur ■

Bundi ■

Panna ■

Rewa ■

BIHAR

WEST BENGAL

Kotah ■

Howrah

Udaipur ■

● Jabalpur

MAIKALA RANGE

Jamshedpur ●

● Calcutta

RANN OF KUTCH

Dungarpur ■

● Bhopal

KUTCH

GUJARAT

● Ahmadabad

Indore ■

VINDHYA RANGE

MADHYA PRADESH

Mahandadi

Kutch ■ **Morvi** ■

Baroda ■

SATPURA RANGE

BAY OF BENGAL

GULF OF KUTCH

Wankaner ■

ORISSA

Porbandar ■

KATHIAWAR

● Surat

GULF OF
CAMBAY

● Nagpur

ARABIAN SEA

MAHARASHTRA

Bombay ●

● Poona

Sholapur ●

Hyderabad ■

EASTERN GHATS

Kolhapur ■

ANDHRA
PRADESH

WESTERN GHATS

KARNATAKA

THE DECCAN

● Madras

Bangalore ■

Mysore ■

NILGIRI HILLS

Ootacamund ■

TAMIL NADU

PALK STRAIT

KERALA

GULF OF
MANNAR

SRI LANKA

Trivandrum ●

0 50 100 150 200 250 300 miles

The marking of international boundaries is not authoritative

············ State boundaries

GLOSSARY

asha   a Rajput potion

caravanserai   an inn for caravans

chaklu   a territorial subdivision

chaori   a yak-tail, used as royal insignia

chatri   site of a cremation

chowie   corrupt spelling of above

chunam   polished lime plaster

dacoit   a robber

gadi   throne

ghat   a steep place, either a hill or the steps leading to a bathing place

gole   a military formation

guru   teacher

haveli   (in this usage) a town-house

holi   spring festival

hookah   pipe for smoking marijuana, tobacco, etc

howdah   canopied seat carried by elephant

jali   carved stone screenwork

jeeroh   a spice

johar   ritual self-sacrifice

lakh   100,000

mardaana   male quarters

maund   a measure of weight

misl   militia

morchal   fan or fly-whisk made of peacocks' feathers

mulki   term used to distinguish the natives of Hyderabad

nazar   gift or offering

pallia   stone commemorating an act of bravery

pan   betel leaf, flavoured by various additions and eaten as a digestive or as a sweet, particularly on ceremonial occasions.

panihari   a water-carrier

pankha   fan

purdah   seclusion of women

saka   fight to the death

sambhar   a wild deer

sari   very long, narrow piece of cloth swathed around the body

serai   inn

shikara   canoe

suttee   ritual suicide, generally on the part of a widow

verandah   porch or portico, sometimes partly enclosed, along the outside of a building

zenana   female quarters